June 2004

Dear Dad -

I picked this up and thought of you!

(I Read it, too ♡)

Enjoy -

Happy 78th -

I Love You -

LISA

WISDOM
OF OUR
FATHERS

WISDOM
OF OUR
FATHERS

Timeless Life
Lessons on
Health, Wealth,
God, Golf, Fear,
Fishing, Sex,
Serenity, Laughter,
and Hope

JOE KITA

Daybreak Books
An imprint of Rodale Books
Emmaus, Pennsylvania

Jacket and Interior Designer: Kristen Morgan Downey
Jacket Photographer: Betsy Cullen/Photonica
Interior Photographer: Richard Corman

Library of Congress Cataloging-in-Publication Data

Kita, Joe.
    Wisdom of our fathers : timeless life lessons on health, wealth, God, golf, fear, fishing, sex, serenity, laughter, and hope / Joe Kita.
        p.   cm.
    ISBN 1–57954–041–4 hardcover
    1. Men—Quotations, maxims, etc.   2. Fathers—Quotations, maxims, etc.   3. Life—Quotations, maxims, etc.   I. Title.
PN6084.M4K58   1999
305.31—dc21   99–17997

Distributed to the book trade by St. Martin's Press

2   4   6   8   10   9   7   5   3   1   hardcover

Visit us on the Web at www.rodalebooks.com or call us
toll-free at (800) 848-4735

---- OUR PURPOSE ----

> *"We publish books that empower
> people's minds and spirits."*

FOR MY CHILDREN, PAUL AND CLAIRE

In case we never get around to discussing things,
it's all in here.

Contents

Introduction

I am still waiting for my father to talk to me about sex and success, money and marriage, religion and raising kids. Since he died in 1991, I guess I don't have much chance of ever benefiting from all of the lessons he learned in life. It's not that he was a bad dad; he was just a quiet one. Even in the best father-son relationships, there's an uncomfortable familiarity that inhibits us from talking like friends.

It's not that our fathers have too little to say to us, but rather too much. Some of them fought the Nazis and struggled through the Depression. They loved women, lost women, raised difficult kids, met every manner of person, good and bad. They witnessed the trajectory of their own careers and lots of others; watched heroes, fads, and politicians come and go; learned what's important and what's not. They've been so many places we have yet to travel. But since neither father nor son knows where or how to start these conversations, we talk about cars, sports, or the weather instead. The shame of it is, I don't know a man my age who doesn't feel that he's navigating his life without a map. Our fathers may not have all the directions, but they sure know where a lot of the potholes and detours lie.

There's a lot of wisdom out there, if only we can ask and listen.

And that's what I've done. I've talked with 138 wise old dads, ranging in age from 40 to 92. Together, they have 486 off-spring and 8,870 years of combined living experience. I asked them all of the questions I wished I had asked my father. What's the key to happiness? How do you find God? At what point do you stop fearing death? When should you marry, divorce, settle in, move on, speak out, give up? What's the one thing in life I shouldn't miss? Define success. Tell me how to always be in love.

These are big questions—topics that history's greatest philosophers have pondered. But you know what? Every father I asked had answers. Even the one who tended bar in a small town in Virginia for 20 years. Or the venetian blinds manufac-turer in New York City. Or the North Carolina dry cleaner who quit school in the seventh grade.

You won't recognize many names in this book. I purposely didn't interview many celebrities or famous dads, even though publishers pressed me to include lots of them, and it might have made the book sell better. But I suspected, and I found, that there is wisdom in every man, in every father, in *your* father.

And that's true whether you love him or despise him. Some of the men you'll hear from are icons of fatherhood, like the fellow in Arizona with 3 biological, 6 adopted, and 18 foster kids. Other dads, however, are no longer even acknowledged by their children, who will no doubt be shocked by their portrayal and inclusion here. But losing a child's love often teaches the hardest lessons. These men know how to do it right, if only because they've done it wrong.

I've had many joyful moments while compiling this book. In fact, because of the unusual conversation we shared, I think of each featured dad as being a father, in some small way, to me. And I have a feeling, a hope, that each one thinks of me as being a bit of a son. I asked for advice, and they tried to help. That's all it takes. If a veritable stranger and I can create a bond like this, just think what you and your father might accomplish on an en-tire Sunday afternoon.

What's sad is that most dads I talked to had never been asked these big questions. We have a tremendous natural resource that's being squandered only because we lack courage and fear intimacy. Most of us take our fathers for granted, and after they're gone, we're left with vague examples to interpret rather than specific words to act upon. I know firsthand the struggle and regret of that. This book is an attempt to help you avoid the same situation and, if you can't because your father is already gone, maybe it will at least plug some of the void.

The book is organized into nine chapters, each dealing with one of the big, unspoken aspects of life. Each begins with a story, what my father taught me, even though he never once addressed the topic in words. Then comes the best advice from the fathers I spoke with, their most insightful quotes on every difficult but vital subject. Interspersed are profiles of 15 noteworthy dads who, because of some unique aspect of their lives, might have something special to contribute to yours.

In addition, you'll find special sections of quotes from my father's journal throughout the book. These are from a journal that he kept when he was young but that I only came to notice on his bookshelf once he was dead. This journal turned out to hold all the advice that he thought wise, yet for some reason never thought to tell me. None of the quotes are original. He merely transcribed those words from others that impressed him. Some I was able to attribute; others I could not. But I don't think that matters much. It's the wisdom they hold that's important.

I don't know how many answers you'll find here. But if you come across even one, just realize that your old man probably has many more. All you have to do is ask him.

Chapter 1

Growing Old
and Staying Young

My father taught me about longevity and health by dying young after never taking care of himself. He was 61 years old when they carried him out of the house in a black body bag, just like in the movies. The coroner shook his head and said that it was a heart attack—an unfortunate script that's played out in little square houses all over the country every day. At least he didn't suffer, the coroner said, since it happened while he slept.

"I'm sorry, but there was *nothing anyone could do.*"

In the months that followed, those last four words echoed in my mind like the bugle over Arlington. Part of it was anger at watching my father carried out like a sack of early-morning trash. Part of it was remorse at never getting the chance to say good-bye or thanks, and really mean it. But part of it was simple, selfish terror—the midnight sound of that thick zipper closing over me—as if this, too, was my genetic destiny.

It was this fear that finally pushed me into a doctor's office a year later for a complete physical exam. I was 32, and for the first time, I was aware of my crumbling invincibility. But the physician mentioned something that instantly made me stop feeling sorry and scared, something so simple yet profound that I couldn't believe I hadn't realized it sooner. "Your heart is a muscle just like any other," he said. "You can beef it up with exercise, or you can let it get scrawny and weak. You have that power."

You have that power.

It's these four words that echo in my mind as I lace up my running shoes on a cold winter morning when others my age are content in their slippers. There *is* something that can be done so that my life doesn't end like my father's.

Richard Ford, the Pulitzer prize–winning novelist, once said that "the best thing a father could do for his son is die." I used to puzzle at the wisdom of this, until it happened to me, and now I realize that in death, my father is finally saying all those things to me that he never got around to in life. Or maybe it's just that he has finally gotten my attention and I'm listening, no longer complacent at his existence and the many examples that he set.

I often recall now the last time I saw him alive. It was a late-October Sunday, the leaves tinged with brown, and the air crisp in a way that made you shiver if you stood still too long. We were standing in my driveway, not talking, just standing, in a momentary suspension of time. He had just returned the kids from an afternoon outing, and they had scattered like those same leaves in the autumn wind. So we were alone, a last chance for what I did not realize. And I looked at him and saw, perhaps for the first time, an old man, even though he was but 61. His face was pale, his eyes were slate gray, and his pants hung about his waist as if they were drying on some lonely clothesline. He'd had the flu all week, but being the ex-Marine that he was, he wouldn't surrender to it. No doctor, no medicine, just a clench of the teeth and a sergeant's resolve.

"You look like hell," is what I said to him.

"Thanks," is what he sarcastically replied.

Then he slowly got into his car and drove away. I gave him a cursory wave and shivered, I thought then, at the October chill. But now, I think something primitive inside me knew that this had been our manly farewell. This was the last time I would see my father alive.

The heart attack came the following dawn. My mother was too distressed to agree to an autopsy, but the experts surmised that it was prompted by his week-long flu. Like any virus, it had weakened his muscles, including his heart muscle. Later, I found a food diary that he had been keeping in order to help control his weight. It showed that in that final week, he had eaten nothing except a few pieces of fruit, some soup, and peanuts. How foolish. How stupid.

Although a coronary is viciously sudden, you don't ordinarily lose your health in a blinding instant. Pick anyone who has died, except maybe in a fateful accident, and you'll be able to trace their disease just like their family tree. My father used to sit on the sofa in the evening smoking cigarettes, drinking beer, and eating potato chips. He kept everything bottled up inside, just like that beer that he loved. And even though he tended a half-acre garden, he would grow out of breath on a flight of stairs.

I know lots of older guys who screwed up their health but got lucky and survived. I wish my father were one of them because despite how poorly he took care of himself, he was a smart man, and he would have learned. But then, I might not have.

Every morning when I look in the mirror, I see my father looking back. And we stand there together, not talking, just standing, in a momentary suspension of time. Only now I seize the chance. I make sure my face has color, that my eyes are bright and blue. I take a vitamin and check to see that my pants (still size 33) fit like a young man's do. And sometimes I flex and make a muscle because I've been lifting weights three times a week, and then I put my hand across my chest to feel my heart beating strong and steadfast. And that man in the mirror, that young man, smiles back.

"You look great," is what he says to me.

"Thanks," is my heartfelt reply.

And I drive off to work, not so sad and distracted anymore, because I realize that a large part of me is my father, and I've made him healthy once more.

A STUBBORN EXISTENCE

"The best way to play the aging game is to concede nothing. Never make it easy for yourself. Should your body suggest that it is too old for this effort, say 'Nonsense!' Should your mind decide that it is too late to learn new tricks, say 'Balderdash!' Should your soul say that it needs a respite from duty and obligation, say 'Rubbish!'

"In time, we will all depart. What we must avoid is to have our actual leaving precede that departure—to die, in effect, before we die, to live out our years in joyless, dependent existence, our body and mind and soul already waiting for us on the other side of the divide."

—GEORGE SHEEHAN, M.D. (1918–1993), AUTHOR, RUNNER, PHILOSOPHER, AND FATHER TO 12

THE CHILD WITHIN

"In general, most people think of old age as a frightening thing. Old people look the way we never want to look. As it happens, I feel perfectly natural at every age I'm at. No one ever told me how little you change inside. One's 12-year-old self and one's present self feel exactly the same."

—WILFRID SHEED, 68, AUTHOR OF *IN LOVE WITH DAYLIGHT*, SURVIVOR OF POLIO, ADDICTION, AND CANCER, AND FATHER TO THREE

WATCHING THE SCALE

"Weigh yourself every day. The biggest health risk for adults is weight gain, and since you cannot sense a three- to five-pound increase, you have to monitor it daily. When you step on the scale, compare what you're seeing today to yesterday, this week to last week, this month to last month. If your weight is up, then you'll know immediately to go into portion control or increase physical activity."

—GEORGE BLACKBURN, M.D., PH.D., 60, DIRECTOR OF A MAJOR NUTRITION AND MEDICAL CENTER AND FATHER TO FOUR

WHAT'S EATING YOU?

"If you don't have some way to identify and deal with your emotions, it can lead to drinking too much, driving too fast, getting into trouble at work, or, in the long-term, developing stress-related heart problems. Try to notice when something is bothering you or if you're distracted, unable to concentrate, or have butterflies in your stomach. Then take the next available moment, sit quietly, and try to tune in to that sensation. Ask yourself what has happened recently to make you feel that way. When you know what it is, then you can do something about it. Realize that it's never shameful to feel."

—RON LEVANT, ED.D., 54, PSYCHOLOGIST AND FATHER TO ONE

THE DIGNITY OF HEALTH

"Think of your health the same way you do your reputation. If you lose it, you may never get it back."

—VINCE SPERRAZZA, 52, TECHNICIAN AND FATHER TO FOUR

COMBINING UPS AND DOWNS

"In the world today, the most commonly consumed beverage, next to water, is coffee. And the most commonly consumed medicine next to birth control pills is sleeping pills. So the whole planet is gulping coffee in the morning and sleeping pills at night. It's a bizarre balance. There's something wrong with that picture."

—RUBIN NAIMAN, PH.D., 49, CLINICAL HEALTH
PSYCHOLOGIST AND FATHER TO THREE

AN APPOINTMENT WITH YOURSELF

"As the CEO of a substantial company, finding time to exercise three or four days a week was the most difficult thing in the world. I finally learned to treat it like another appointment. I even told my secretary to schedule it."

—JOE SCIORTINO, 66, RETIRED EXECUTIVE AND FATHER TO TWO

From My Father's Journal

"As long as you live, keep learning how to live." —SENECA

❧

"Hardening of the heart ages people more quickly than hardening of the arteries."

❧

"We grow too soon old and too late smart."
—PENNSYLVANIA DUTCH PROVERB

❧

"It is with life as with a play—it matters not how long the action is spun out, but how good the acting is." —SENECA

❧

"Fresh air keeps the doctor poor." —DANISH PROVERB

❧

"Avarice in old age is foolish; for what can be more absurd than to increase our provisions for the road the nearer we approach to our journey's end?"
—MARCUS TULLIUS CICERO

❧

"Fat men are more likely to die suddenly than the slender." —HIPPOCRATES

❧

"Cheerfulness and content are great beautifiers and famous preservers of youthful looks." —CHARLES DICKENS

LETHAL STUPIDITY

"Only about 1 person in 10 dies of old age. The rest commit what I call slow suicide by smoking, drinking, taking drugs, being promiscuous, not exercising, and, worst of all, overeating. I don't do any of these things, and I plan on living to be 200. If you're smart, you can, too."

—MILLER QUARLES, 83, PRESIDENT OF THE CURING OLD-AGE DISEASE SOCIETY, GEOPHYSICIST, AND FATHER TO THREE

CONTAGIOUS AGING

"Never hang around people who use age as an excuse. It's like yawning. If you're with someone who does it, pretty soon you're doing it too."

—HARRY SCOTT, 65, USA MASTERS BODYBUILDING CHAMP AND FATHER TO THREE

A THREE-LEGGED STOOL

"Think of your health and well-being as a three-legged stool. One leg is pharmaceuticals or medicine. The second leg is routine medical care or surgery. The third, and increasingly more vital, leg is self-care. This comprises nutrition, exercise, stress management, and even your belief system or spirituality. You can't be healthy without three strong legs."

—HERBERT BENSON, M.D., 63, PRESIDENT OF A MIND/BODY MEDICAL INSTITUTE, AUTHOR OF TIMELESS HEALING, AND FATHER TO TWO

SUPERMAN SYNDROME

"Don't be reckless with your health. When I was young, I thought I was God Almighty. Then I had a heart attack at age 34. My doctor told me I had 'Superman Syndrome.' He says that when a guy feels good, he thinks he's Superman. He only comes to see the doctor when the kryptonite gets him."
—RALPH HAAS, 63, RETIRED RADIO DISC JOCKEY, AUTHOR, AND FATHER TO TWO

A LITTLE OLIVE OIL

"Olive oil—a tablespoonful at each meal—is a worthwhile item of diet for general health. The olive tree lives for thousands of years. There may be something in the sap that promotes health and longevity. The Italians thrive on it."
—J. I. RODALE (1898–1971), PUBLISHER, PHILOSOPHER, AND FATHER TO THREE

HOW TO BEAT STRESS (PART 1)

"Stress is the biggest cause of health problems among the male patients I see. For 70 to 80 percent, stress causes or worsens physical problems such as migraines, irritable bowel syndrome, and ulcers. But it's not that difficult to learn how to control stress. You can literally unplug yourself with three breaths. You don't have to close the door or turn off the lights. Just sit where you are, even while you're talking to someone, and take three slow, deep abdominal breaths to calm yourself. Try it right now. Do it whenever you're feeling hassled during the day."
—WOODSON MERRELL, M.D., 50, INTEGRATIVE PHYSICIAN, PROFESSOR OF MEDICINE, AND FATHER TO TWO

KEEP WONDERING

"The day your curiosity dies, your life is over."
—ROD STEIGER, 73, OSCAR-WINNING ACTOR
AND FATHER TO ONE

INVENTORY THE WAREHOUSE

"Get a thorough physical exam every 18 months. My father did that. In fact, he had a string of doctors he'd go to. I used to think he was a hypochondriac. But I realize now that he was just taking inventory. He wanted to know where he was at. And while he was testing himself, he was also testing doctors. That was wise. He lived to be 84."
—JOE DRAKE (1922–1998), ATTORNEY AND FATHER TO FOUR

THE MYTH OF GETTING FIT

"Saying you want to get in shape, look better, or lose weight is setting yourself up for failure, because you'll never achieve any of these things to your satisfaction. You'll never be fit enough, attractive enough, or thin enough. To make an exercise program work, you need specific functional goals, both short- and long-range. This could mean training for a five-mile race three months from now or adopting a walking program so that you'll be able to get around on your own 50 years from now. An exercise program without specific goals will never succeed."
—JAMES GLINN, 54, PHYSICAL THERAPIST AND FATHER TO TWO

FREE HYPERTENSION MEDICINE

"It's my belief that if you smile in life, you'll keep your blood pressure normal."
—JOSEPH McFADDEN (1922–1997), DIPLOMAT, PROFESSOR
OF JOURNALISM, AND FATHER TO FIVE

Make Sure You Can Touch Your Toes

Aging is a deterioration of connective tissue. The stiffness, shrinkage, and drying up of aging occur directly in that great web of fiber that ties us together. What exercise does is resist this stiffening. Age is what makes it tight, movement is what keeps it loose. If you can't stay young, stay loose."
—John Jerome, 66, author of 10 books, including *The Elements of Effort*, and father to three

The Joy of Doing

"Freud said what's important in life is love and work. But too much of one and not enough of the other causes problems. The people who I find are healthiest and happiest are those who get up every morning and can't wait to go forth—those who love their work."
—Paul Rosch, M.D., 69, president of the American Institute of Stress and father to six

The Enemy

"Your enemy is gravity. Without your even noticing, it's constantly pulling your muscles and skin toward the ground. It's busy kicking your butt. To withstand it, make your body resilient with exercise and low-fat fuel. Never forget that the body is the only machine that the more you use it, the longer it will last. Make it your goal to wage war on gravity and win."
—Harry Scott, 65, USA Masters Bodybuilding champ and father to three

HOW TO BEAT STRESS (PART 2)

"Vacations are very important for reducing stress. Anybody with a busy job should take two or three breaks a year for at least a week at a time. You need seven days to decompress and, ideally, another seven to really feel like you're on vacation. Also, try to do something interesting and active that takes you out of your routine and exposes you to new things. Don't just go lie on some beach. Try kayaking, mountain biking, hiking . . ."
—WOODSON MERRELL, M.D., 50, INTEGRATIVE PHYSICIAN, PROFESSOR OF MEDICINE, AND FATHER TO TWO

THE VALUE OF COOL

"I've had a few hairy experiences in my life. I survived three plane crashes, got blown out of a foxhole during World War II, and was bayoneted in Korea. And I had five heart attacks between 1979 and 1988. After the last one, I had open-heart surgery and was on the table for 15 hours. But that was years ago, and I feel great now. In fact, I bench-pressed 225 pounds five times on my 69th birthday. People call me an inspiration, but I've always just tried to keep a cool head. If you get too excited, the adrenaline starts pumping too fast, and you do stupid things."
—SAM JERZAK (1924–1995), 26-YEAR ARMY VETERAN AND FATHER TO SIX

YOUR TO-DO LIST

"The fitness formula for the body is quite simple. Pick your activity, then do 30 minutes at a comfortable pace four times a week. Follow a similar program for the mind. Pick your activity and then do it for 45 minutes, four times a week. Fitness may take time, but it makes time as well."
—GEORGE SHEEHAN, M.D. (1918–1993), AUTHOR, RUNNER, PHILOSOPHER, AND FATHER TO 12

EVEN EINSTEIN SLEPT

"A lot of men wear sleep deprivation as a badge of courage. Dozens of CEOs pride themselves on sleeping just four to five hours a night. What happens, though, is your judgment disappears and your perception is impaired. Three-Mile Island, Chernobyl, and the *Exxon Valdez* are all examples of sleep-related accidents. To remain healthy and be at your peak, you need about 8 hours of sleep per day. Einstein slept 10 hours."

—RUBIN NAIMAN, PH.D., 49, CLINICAL HEALTH
PSYCHOLOGIST AND FATHER TO THREE

DON'T BE A SPECTATOR

"Instead of sitting in the stands and watching your kids play sports, get out there with them. I started figure skating when I was 40. I saw all these other fathers and mothers standing around the rink, waiting for their kids, keeping their hands warm wrapped around hot cups of coffee. I thought, what a waste of time. So I decided to take lessons with my kids."

—JOE DRAKE (1922–1998), ATTORNEY AND FATHER TO FOUR

LOOKS CAN KILL

"There's a difference between staying young in spirit and staying young in appearance. Most people think that appearance is the important thing, and most of their effort and money goes toward preserving it. I say, don't pay much attention to that. It's good health and good spirit that really keeps you young."

—GORDY SHIELDS, 80, RETIRED HIGH SCHOOL TEACHER
AND COLLEGE COUNSELOR, COMPETITIVE CYCLIST,
AND FATHER TO THREE

From My Father's Journal

"He is the best physician who is the most ingenious inspirer of hope." —SAMUEL TAYLOR COLERIDGE

❧

"Forty is the old age of youth; fifty is the youth of old age." —VICTOR HUGO

❧

"Curiosity is one of the most permanent and certain characteristics of a vigorous intellect."

❧

"Age should not have its face lifted but rather teach the world to admire wrinkles as the etchings of experience and the firm lines of character."

❧

"Iron rusts from disuse, stagnant water loses its purity and in cold weather, becomes frozen; even so does inaction sap the vigors of the mind."

❧

"The survival of the fittest is the ageless law of nature, but the fittest are rarely the strong. The fittest are those endowed with the qualifications for adaptation, the ability to accept the inevitable and conform to the unavoidable, to harmonize with existing or changing conditions."

❧

"Youth is a quality, not a matter of circumstances."

MIND AEROBICS

"Never stop learning. Otherwise, your mind will become stagnant. I retired in 1981, but I still take classes to keep myself sharp. Photography, history, political science, music, whatever. It's better than just sitting and watching television."
—IRA COLEMAN, 89, RETIRED FEDERAL NARCOTICS AGENT, THE OLDEST STUDENT AT HIS LOCAL COMMUNITY COLLEGE, AND FATHER TO THREE

LIFE'S NUMBER ONE GOAL

"Make good health your prime goal in life because without it, you won't be able to achieve any other goals."
—JOSEPH McFADDEN (1922–1997), DIPLOMAT, PROFESSOR OF JOURNALISM, AND FATHER TO FIVE

HOW TO BEAT STRESS (PART 3)

"The most stressful time in a man's life is his late thirties and early forties. Younger men expect pressure, and they cope. But middle-aged men are generally less optimistic because they're realizing that the path to success is rockier than imagined. Plus, they're raising families, and financial burdens are setting in. When a stressful situation arises, ask yourself how important it really is. Rate it on a scale of 1 to 10. If it's not a 9 or a 10, then you don't have to worry. It helps keep things in perspective."
—ALLEN ELKIN, PH.D., 56, DIRECTOR OF A STRESS MANAGEMENT COUNSELING CENTER AND FATHER TO TWO

KEEP YOUR MOTOR RUNNING

"If you exercise consistently, that's the pot of gold that'll give you another 20 years. The human body is the greatest machine of all, because it can keep getting better."
—GEORGE FOREMAN, 50, WORLD'S OLDEST HEAVYWEIGHT BOXING CHAMPION AND FATHER TO NINE

You Can

"Be positive, even when the news is grim. I lost a lung to cancer at age 36, and the doctors told my wife that I had three months to live. But I fooled them. I spent 2½ years in chemotherapy—the worst 2½ years of my life—but I beat it. I had four kids and a wonderful wife, and I didn't want to leave them. When you're fighting something that big for that long, it's the little victories you have to focus on. Like when they took me to the hospital, my wife wanted me to go in a wheelchair. But I said no. They may have to wheel me out, but they're not wheeling me in."

—FRANK VIVIANI, 60, CANCER SURVIVOR AND FATHER TO FOUR

Health Drips Away

"Most everyone starts out with a great physical body, but as we go through life, we tend to screw it up. Think of that next cigarette you're about to have, or that next drink, or that next cheeseburger, as drops of water falling into a bucket. It takes a long time, but eventually, if you're not careful, your bucket will fill up."

—BILL BELL, 75, RETIRED MARKETING EXECUTIVE WHO HAS COMPETED IN MORE THAN 200 TRIATHLONS AND 152 MARATHONS SINCE AGE 53, AND FATHER TO THREE

How to Know When You're in Shape

"My definition of fitness is to be able to carry out all of the activities in life that you desire, plus have a physical reserve at the end of the day to do something besides lie down and flip the remote. If you can do all that, if you're functional, then you're fit. It doesn't matter if you have great abs or can bench-press your body weight. Those things have nothing to do with real life."

—JAMES GLINN, 54, PHYSICAL THERAPIST AND FATHER TO TWO

TAKING PILLS

"If you're taking different medications, pay attention to how they interact. Ask your doctor and pharmacist specifically about it. I spent two years taking all kinds of pills. The doctors would give me something for my pain and then, if it made me jittery, they'd give me something else for that. I was either headed up or down on prescription medicine, and I finally decided that I wasn't going to live that kind of life. I got rid of just about everything, and today, I feel healthier and I'm more active because of it."

—RALPH HAAS, 63, RETIRED RADIO DISC JOCKEY, AUTHOR, AND FATHER TO TWO

WHY MEN GET FAT

"Men's metabolisms start slowing down in their mid- to late thirties. So if at 40 you're eating the same way you did at 30, you're guaranteed to put on weight. It's that simple. To compensate, it's crucial that you exercise more and eat less as you age."

—WOODSON MERRELL, M.D., 50, INTEGRATIVE PHYSICIAN, PROFESSOR OF MEDICINE, AND FATHER TO TWO

THE BENEFITS OF BUSY

"If you don't like to exercise, or if you just can't find the time, then at least keep busy. I've been working since I was 14. I worked on the railroad for 37½ years. I started out as a gandy dancer, digging ties and doing the dirty work. Even after I retired, I kept active. I mean, I'm going all the time. I work around the village here. I run the backhoe for them. I run the grader. I haul stone. And just this weekend, I put a new roof on the house. Keeping busy is the best thing for your health."

—WILL HESS, 70, RETIRED RAILROAD WORKER AND FATHER TO FOUR

Pump Up This Muscle

"For a life with more life in it—more capacity—train your heart. A well-trained heart pumps more blood with each stroke, accomplishing more work with less energy expenditure. By beating more slowly, it gets a chance to rest. The more it rests, the stronger it gets."

—John Jerome, 66, author of 10 books, including
The Elements of Effort, and father to three

The Secret of Youth

"The secret to staying young is to be interested, truly interested, in everything happening around you."

—Charles VanBuskirk (1917–1998), quality control
engineer and father to two

Four-Cylinder Living

"Hang out with people in the slow lane. Take the time to learn, make friends, appreciate things. The fast life is over quick."

—Rudy Sanchez, 85, former nightclub entertainer
and father to one

Those Payday Blues

"Nothing will make you older than working at a job that you hate year after year, just trying to keep the money coming in so you can pay the bills. You have to be able to get up each day and look forward to what you're doing. If you hate life, it depresses your immune system. The thing that makes youth so exciting is that everything is new. If you're doing the same thing every day, then everything is old, and you become old."

—Fred Matheny, 53, writer, former English teacher,
and father to one

THE POWER OF PLAY

"Being young at heart is simply a matter of doing those things that you enjoy. Whether it's bowling, golf, tennis, or something else, you're young when you're doing them."
—BILL DEWEY, 62, FORMER PARTNER IN A GREETING CARD COMPANY, SALESMAN, AND FATHER TO TWO

Robert N. Butler, M.D., 68

If there's anyone you'd expect to be vibrant, inspirational, and wise at an older age, it's Robert N. Butler, M.D. Founding director of the National Institute on Aging, Pulitzer Prize–winning author of *Why Survive? Being Old In America*, CEO of the International Longevity Center, and nationally recognized expert on senior sex, he has made an illustrious career out of studying life's progression. And although he's sensitive to sounding like he has all of the answers, Butler seems to be aging gracefully. His cholesterol count is 150, he walks regularly on a treadmill and in New York City's Central Park, he has never had any major health problems, and after rearing three children in one marriage, he has an 18-year-old daughter from a second.

EARLY RETIREMENT: "Those young men who think about early retirement are in a fantasy world. It's better to think of how you'll remain productive later in life. More people are having three and four careers. Keep learning and, if you retire, retire to something that gives you a sense of purpose. Studies show a relationship between purpose and living longer."

FRIENDSHIP: "Men need to maintain their friends, nourish them, and strive for some of the same intimacy that women have in their friendships. For instance, rather than sending cards, I call each of my friends at Christmas."

HEALTH: "I do all the recommended things: I don't smoke, and I drink alcohol moderately, exercise, take vitamins, eat a low-fat diet, and take an aspirin a day. But health is not just physical. There are two other components: social health, which

has to do with your set of relationships and your friends; and sense of purpose, which I just spoke about. You need all three to be truly healthy."

Fatherhood: "It's important to become friends with your children. You do this by sharing a common interest, treating them as equals, and not taking advantage of your being the older person."

Regrets: "As a gerontologist, I do a lot of listening to older people. Their biggest regret is not what they did but what they failed to do. They regret not standing up for something, not expressing an affection."

Sex: "There are two languages of sex. The first reflects our reproductive function. It's explosive and highly emotional, and it comes naturally. The second language is something you acquire. It involves becoming more sensitive to your partner, more concerned with their needs. It's the secret to having a continuing love affair."

Jim Law (1926–1996)

He was America's fastest man age 65 and older—sort of a Carl Lewis with white hair. Jim Law, a sprinter from Charlotte, North Carolina, held three age-group world records and could run 100 meters in 13 seconds. (Try it sometime.) But even more impressive was the fact that he was once 20 pounds overweight, had a cholesterol count of 322, and smoked more than a pack of cigarettes a day.

A one-time spokesman for the National Senior Sports Organization, this former psychology professor and father to two toured the country talking to elderly Americans about starting again and savoring life.

Staying young: "I don't want to be forever young. We're conditioned by our youth-oriented society to think of incapacity or loss when we think of the elderly. Anytime anything appears that's of merit in the old, we put 'young' on it: 'He's 84 years *young*.' But it's quite all right to be old and competent, old and

creative, old and energetic. Each age is an opportunity, as Longfellow said. I like old. I like wrinkles, measured steps, and a twinkle in the eyes."

HEALTH: "The key to healthy aging is smart eating, smart exercise, and taking charge of your life. The first two are self-explanatory, but that last one has to do with self-efficacy—not losing your mastery, autonomy, and independence. Continue to do things that allow you to engage life vigorously. Don't allow others to take charge of your life. And that includes bucking your doctor when necessary. If he tells you that your difficulties are due to aging, then get another doctor. Many of the deteriorations associated with aging actually stem from disuse, neglect, and inactivity. Life is movement."

SEX: "When I was a kid and I went to the barbershop, I used to hear the old men say, 'I'm not as good as I once was, but I'm as good *once* as I ever was.' Then they'd slap high fives and laugh. I'd laugh, too, even though I didn't know what they were talking about. I do now."

WORK: "So many men put so much energy into their jobs that it produces a breakdown, either emotional or physical. The same thing can result from too much money, too much fun, too much anything that prevents experiencing the diversity of life. Don't put all your energy in one place. Emphasize balance in life and de-emphasize defining yourself by the work you do."

COACHING KIDS: "Introduce your children to sports, but always pull back after they get the hang of it."

WINNING AND LOSING: "What I've learned from competing in this twilight zone is that you need a mature approach to goal-setting. Rather than winning, look for continuous growth. If you do this creatively, you can have a good time. One fellow I know runs in a lot of local races and is almost always last. He says he doesn't compete against the guys in front of him but against the little guy inside of him who says, 'Quit.' You can find victory in unsuspected places, and once you decide that winning isn't everything, you become a winner."

MAKING MISTAKES: "You learn more from failure than you do from success. Pay attention to your mistakes, make the necessary alterations, then try again. Many people are afraid to make mistakes, when in fact, they should welcome them and learn to benefit from them."

BEATING STRESS: "Get a chunk of time in each day that is yours and yours alone, and savor it."

MAKING A COMEBACK: "Traditionally, we look forward to retirement to do an abundance of nothing, but that's not it at all. Here I am almost in my 70s, and I still don't know what I'll do when I grow up. At any age, you can start anything."

REGRETS: "There used to be a special bonding between the old and the young. There were three generations in every household. It's a pity that's still not so. There's so much to be learned. I heard of a Scandinavian country that refuses to build a nursing home unless a nursery is nearby."

BEING THANKFUL: "Thanksgiving is my favorite holiday. It's the least contaminated by commercialism, and it generates appropriate kinds of prayer—prayers of gratitude instead of prayers of petition."

WHATEVER YOU DO, DON'T MISS: "An appreciation of nature. I live in an urban setting, looking at bricks and glass, smelling exhaust. But when I run, I'm out there with trees and birds. Uniting with nature gives you a different sense of self."

FINDING HAPPINESS: "Let the endorphins flow. These hormones are released by the brain under certain circumstances to mask pain and produce euphoria. Exercise is one way to make this happen—runner's high, it's called. But there are other things that release them and produce the same exhilaration and calm. I get it by helping other people, by laughing, and I've heard talk of tears and prayers producing them as well. So let the endorphins flow. You'll feel much, much better."

Chapter 2

Work, Money, and Success

My father lost a lot of money late in his life. In fact, if he hadn't died when he did, he might have eventually lost everything.

He was fascinated with the stock market. Each payday, he bought a few more shares of the company he worked for, AT&T. Some of them he gave to me. He'd show me the certificates, and at my young age, they seemed more ornately official and important than money itself. He'd also show me the tablet upon which he tracked the gradual rise in his stocks' prices. And each year at tax time, he'd even tabulate my net worth, which for a boy was always inspiring, no matter how meager.

When the U.S. government split up AT&T's monopoly, my father received stock in seven new telephone companies, the Baby Bells, as they were called. His tablet was filled with columns and numbers now, most all tracking positively upward. I felt like we were rich. We had a nice house with an in-ground pool. My father bought a new Ford Thunderbird, and later, a black Lincoln. We went out to eat at a sit-down restaurant every Wednesday and grilled filet mignons on Sundays. He insisted that he pay for my college education, that it was his responsibility as a father.

For my wedding, he chartered a bus and filled it with beer

and liquor for our friends and relatives. When I bought my first house, he paid for the sunroom that we built off the back. One Christmas, he gave my wife and me a video camera to help remember our babies. And just before he died, he sent in the deposit for a 10-day Disney World vacation for the entire family.

I was never in dire need of anything. Money was never an issue.

That's why it came as such a shock when the estate lawyer solemnly shook his head and showed my mother and me a bottom line of nearly a quarter of a million dollars of debt. There was a list of 15 credit cards on that tablet now, all at their borrowing limits and all with unpaid principals compounding at 18 to 20 percent interest. And there were margin loans, too—money borrowed against his existing stock at a preferred but still substantial rate.

I'll never fully understand how this happened. I guess he had grown so confident in the market's growth that he had greedily bought more stock with loaned money and then got caught short when it underperformed. It's like a bug being flushed down a toilet. The swirl starts slowly, and it thinks it can escape, but the whirlpool is always intensifying and is ultimately too great.

Death saved him, in a way, from embarrassment and humiliation, from perhaps asking me for money the way I always seemed to be asking him. Luckily, all those credit cards and loans were in his name only, so my mother didn't lose the family house, the life insurance settlement, or her dignity.

Still, it hurt to know that he had failed, that his net worth was even lower than mine, and that during the last years of his life, he had been alone with this torment. Sometimes I wonder if he might have quietly taken his own life. After all, the coroner's survey was quick and perfunctory, and my mother wouldn't allow an autopsy. Despite how sick the thought of suicide makes me feel, that option was a porthole for a trapped and drowning man. He must have seen it. He must have realized that by smartly sacrificing himself, he could escape his creditors, protect his family's future, and still be buried with honor.

These days, I pay off my credit card bills in full each month. And although I still own stock (including some of the AT&T that my father originally gave me), I will never borrow against its value. Within reason, I give my children what they want. We go out to eat at a sit-down restaurant once a week. I intend to pay for their college educations because I believe that's my duty as a dad. We've gone to Disney World three times now. And I suspect they think I'm rich.

Let them have that illusion, like I did of my father. Little minds are more apt to respect the successful. But even if my pockets are empty when I die, I know that they'll still inherit a mountain of wealth. Whether they learn from my examples or my mistakes, it's learning nonetheless. And if I'm not destined to be rich in paper, then at least I can be rich in spirit. My father was that way until the very end. Part of my shock came from how expertly he had covered it all up. His attitude, even in the face of impending bankruptcy, was always worth a million bucks.

Perhaps my dad died a wealthy man, after all. Perhaps I can do the same.

COPY FROM THE BEST

"Find someone whose work you admire and emulate it. Norman Rockwell has been my mentor since I first picked up a crayon. When I was a boy, I would copy and recopy his *Saturday Evening Post* covers. So you can imagine my thrill when I had the privilege of working with him when I became an art director.

"I remember on one of my first visits to his studio in Stockbridge, Massachusetts, I mentioned to him that I thought that the main character in one of his paintings struck the same pose as Michelangelo's *David*. Rockwell smiled, took a puff of his pipe, and said, 'When you copy, copy from the best.'

"I guess I had the right idea when I was a boy."

—JOSEPH CSATARI, 70, COMMERCIAL ILLUSTRATOR
AND FATHER TO THREE

From My Father's Journal

"We judge ourselves by what we think we can do. Others judge us by what we have already done."

❧

"One man with courage makes a majority."
—ANDREW JACKSON

❧

"The mark of the immature man is that he wants to die nobly for a cause, while the mark of a mature man is that he wants to live humbly for one." —WILHELM STEKEL

❧

"Be not afraid of life. Believe that life is worth living, and your belief will help create the fact." —WILLIAM JAMES

❧

"A real home is a shelter from the storms of life, a place to enjoy, a place in which to relax, a place of peace and rest. A true home is the center of all human hopes and ideals. It does not have to be a mansion."
—DR. CLIFFORD R. ANDERSON

❧

"Make friends of your creditors, but never make creditors of your friends." —HENRY A. COURTNEY

❧

"There is something that is much more scarce, something finer far, something rarer than ability. It is the ability to recognize ability." —ELBERT HUBBARD

HAVE A SELF-MARKETING STRATEGY

"When it comes to work, view yourself as an asset. An asset is what a company pays for. It doesn't pay for your name, your background, or your affiliation. It pays you for providing a profit impetus in the next quarter. It's up to you to make sure that you're not sitting in the same job for five years and feeling very comfortable and safe. Instead, you always need to be looking beyond to see if you're still what the company needs to execute its strategic plan. You are responsible for marketing yourself."

—CHARLES KOVAC, 70, RETIRED CORPORATE VICE-PRESIDENT
AND FATHER TO SEVEN

HOW TO LAND YOUR DREAM JOB

"Make a big circle on a piece of typing paper. Put a dot in the center and mark that your dream job—the job that you feel perfectly suited for, based on your education and experience. Now think of other jobs similar to your dream job and make a dot for each of them closer or farther from the center, based on the strength of similarity. Next, draw rings on your circle, like on a dartboard. Start with the ring nearest the center and do a job search on each of the job dots there. If nothing is available, then go to the next circle out, and so on. Eventually, you should land a job that will help you work your way to the bull's-eye."

—DENIS BOYLES, 52, PROFESSOR, WRITER, FARMER,
AND FATHER TO THREE

THE TEST OF TIME

"Success means controlling your own time. If you can gain control over 60 percent of the time in your life, you are really successful."

—ROD STEIGER, 73, OSCAR-WINNING ACTOR
AND FATHER TO ONE

TAKE MORE WATER-COOLER BREAKS

"Repetition and routine make the neural circuits tired, whatever the nature of the task. The only way to get a fresh start is to use different circuits for a while. Shooting the breeze around the water cooler may drive bosses crazy, but it shouldn't. It's exactly enough break to resharpen manual dexterity or wits or vision or whatever it is that goes stale when one sticks too long to a task, to say nothing about maintaining proper hydration, which is more of a factor in efficiency and consistent performance than most employers dream."

—JOHN JEROME, 66, AUTHOR OF 10 BOOKS, INCLUDING
THE ELEMENTS OF EFFORT, AND FATHER TO THREE

SELLING YOURSELF SHORT

"Those around me assume that functioning adequately means that you are normal. But one can function adequately while using only about 10 percent of one's potential. We have this tendency to sell ourselves short. We do it daily. We do not believe that we can become athletes, so we become spectators. We do not believe that we can become heroes, so we become followers. We do not believe that we can become philosophers, so we never find our truth."

—GEORGE SHEEHAN, M.D. (1918-1993), AUTHOR, RUNNER,
PHILOSOPHER, AND FATHER TO 12

THE FIVE ELEMENTS OF SUCCESS

"To succeed in business and in life, you need discipline, determination, and dedication, plus the tenacity of a bulldog. But it has to be tempered with patience so that you don't get overly ambitious and stressed."

—MORRIS BRUCHES, 76, RETIRED VENETIAN BLINDS
MANUFACTURER AND FATHER TO TWO

MAKING A DIFFERENCE

"In the end, it's important for a man to feel that he's made a difference somehow in the work that he's done. Whether you're a plumber, a carpenter, a teacher, or a Wall Street person, success is the sense that you've made a positive difference."

—GEORGE BOOTH, 78, RETIRED MINISTER
AND FATHER TO FOUR

SECRET BUSINESS WEAPON

"Collect punchlines. Good joke tellers are envied and in short supply."

—JOSEPH McFADDEN (1922–1997), DIPLOMAT, PROFESSOR
OF JOURNALISM, AND FATHER TO FIVE

SAVING MONEY

"The secret to saving is to pretend that you went out and bought lunch or had a few drinks, then put that same amount of money away and forget about it. That's how I survived the Depression. I remember I got up to $60 in savings once, and I thought I was rich."

—RUBEN DOMINGUEZ, 86, RETIRED MANUAL LABORER
AND FATHER TO FOUR

WHEN YOU'LL PEAK

"When you're young, you have lots of energy and no experience. When you're very old, you have lots of experience and no energy. During your fifties is when the two balance out. That's when your earning power and achievements are at their highest."

—DAVID BENDANIEL, PH.D., 67, PROFESSOR
OF ENTREPRENEURSHIP AND FATHER TO TWO

THE ART OF THE GOLF DEAL

"The golf course is one of the best places to do business, only there's a strategy for doing it successfully. During the first six holes, get to know each other—likes, dislikes, family life. During the middle six holes, shift the conversation to business—how his is doing, what keeps him up at night, your proposal. During the final six holes, try to move the deal along—strengthen the pitch, talk specifics, test the waters. Then, in the bar afterward—the 19th hole—press for a future date to finalize the deal."

—DAN WEILBAKER, PH.D., 50, PROFESSOR OF SALES
AND FATHER TO TWO (GOLFERS)

DIG THE PERFECT DITCH

"Whatever it is you're doing, do a good job. Be sure that all the bases are covered. If you have to dig a ditch, be sure that the corners are straight, the water runs through it, and no one will fall in. This is the attitude."

—HENRY IKEMOTO, 74, RETIRED PROBATION OFFICER
AND FATHER TO FOUR

HOW TO NEGOTIATE

"When you're negotiating, don't go for the jugular. Keep a fall-back position and be able to let your adversary reach his fall-back position. Everyone has one. In diplomatic situations, strength is knowing where it is and being able to reach it with a smile."

—JOSEPH MCFADDEN (1922–1997), DIPLOMAT, PROFESSOR
OF JOURNALISM, AND FATHER TO FIVE

From My Father's Journal

"Every now and then go away, have a little relaxation, for when you come back to your work your judgement will be surer since to remain constantly at work will cause you to lose power of judgement. Go some distance away because then the work appears smaller, and more of it can be taken in at a glance, a lack of harmony or proportion is more readily seen."
—Leonardo da Vinci

❦

"With all thy getting, get understanding."
—Malcolm S. Forbes

❦

"Confidence is the companion of success."

❦

"Training means learning the rules. Experience means learning the exceptions."

❦

"Use what talents you possess: The woods would be very silent if no birds sang except those that sang best."

❦

"Those who dare to teach or lead must never cease to learn."

❦

"You may succeed when others do not believe in you, but never when you do not believe in yourself."

FINDING YOUR NICHE

"What do you feel passionate about? What do you have fun doing? I believe that what you love is what you were made to do, and what you were made to do is what you have an aptitude to do. Have the courage to admit what you love, and your genius will burst through."

—DAVID MCNALLY, 52, MOTIVATIONAL BUSINESS CONSULTANT, AUTHOR OF *THE EAGLE'S SECRET*, AND FATHER TO FIVE

BEING PUNCTUAL

"If you want to build a successful career, start by being on time for your job."

—BENNIE MANCINO, 77, RETIRED INDUSTRIAL WORKER, UNION CHAIRMAN, AND FATHER TO THREE

THE DANGER OF FLATTERY

"Never let yourself be flattered into a job. If you're offered, say, a company presidency somewhere, no doubt you'll be impressed. But on closer examination, accepting it may be the worst thing you could do for yourself and your family. Nevertheless, sometimes the flattery of it will take you there anyway. It's real tempting when it happens. You have to be careful."

—B. G. STEPHENS, PH.D., 63, COLLEGE ADMINISTRATOR, CHEMIST, AND FATHER TO FOUR

MONEY AND HAPPINESS

"People are always saying that money isn't important, but I think that it is important. Happiness is great, of course, but if you have a little money, you can be a little happier."

—BOB CHRISTMAN, 64, RETIRED SCHOOLTEACHER AND FATHER TO FOUR

Asking Dad for a Loan

"Do not under any circumstances borrow money from your father if you're over the age of 32. If you need parental cash and you're older than that, it had better be for a business investment in an office condo or something. If it's cash for groceries and bills, you're in bad shape if you have to ask the old man. But you're in worse shape if he says, 'Sure.' Delaying personal maturity is far more expensive than delaying maturity on a CD to avoid going to the First Bank of Dad."
—Denis Boyles, 52, professor, writer, farmer, and father to three

Why You Should Read More Robert Frost

"I used to teach poetry. And the thing that I always told the kids when they said they hated it was that if you think of basketball, gymnastics, sprinting, or any athletic event, what you're seeing is people using their bodies to the absolute maximum that they can be used in an activity. And that's neat. When you look at a poem, what you're seeing is a human being using words and ideas to the absolute maximum. And that's important because the thing that really separates man from the rest of animal creation is our ability to use language. And if you understand poetry, then you understand how to express yourself. You understand how to sway people. You understand how to use words. And that's a very powerful skill."
—Fred Matheny, 53, writer, former English teacher, and father to one

How to Make an Impression

"To set yourself up for success, under-promise and over-deliver."
—Ed Shea, 53, relationship counselor and father to two

YOUR MOST PRODUCTIVE TIME

"Most of us have become so action-oriented that we don't put aside time to consider what it all means, who we are, and where we're headed. In contrast, many successful people tell me that their most productive time of all, the time when they get their best ideas and biggest insights, is when they close their doors and allow themselves to contemplate and ponder. Try it sometime."

—DAVID MCNALLY, 52, MOTIVATIONAL BUSINESS CONSUL-
TANT, AUTHOR OF *THE EAGLE'S SECRET*, AND FATHER TO FIVE

CUTTING CORNERS

"There are no shortcuts in life. If you take shortcuts in life, you'll cut life short."

—GORDY SHIELDS, 80, RETIRED HIGH SCHOOL TEACHER
AND COLLEGE COUNSELOR, COMPETITIVE CYCLIST,
AND FATHER TO THREE

DESK JOBS ARE DEATH JOBS

"The best jobs involve traveling and learning. My first job offer was keeping track of boxcars at a major railroad in St. Louis, sitting at a desk looking at three-by-five cards. But I decided I didn't want to do anything like that; it looked awful. So even though it paid well—$350 a week—I didn't take it. Instead, I became a soap salesman. It paid less, but it gave me a chance to get out and see and do things in the community."

—BOB MCCOY, 71, CURATOR OF THE MUSEUM
OF QUESTIONABLE MEDICAL DEVICES AND FATHER TO THREE

THE EVOLUTION OF WEALTH

"Money never becomes meaningless, but it becomes less significant every day."

—ALFRED WILLIAMS, 64, FORMER PRESIDENT COUNTY JUDGE
AND FATHER TO THREE

THE BEST TIME TO START A BUSINESS

"Thirty-five is the best age to strike out on your own. If you wait much longer than that, you begin to get weighed down with responsibilities—children, mortgage payments—and you start settling into a certain lifestyle. Earlier than that, and you usually don't know enough people or have enough experience to be successful."

—DAVID BENDANIEL, PH.D., 67, PROFESSOR
OF ENTREPRENEURSHIP AND FATHER TO TWO

STAND FOR SOMETHING

"I heard a song a little while back that said, 'You got to stand for something, or you'll fall for anything.' I thought that was pretty true. Don't be a wimp. Never go along just to get along."

—BILL BAKER, 68, RETIRED MAINTENANCE TECHNICIAN
AND FATHER TO TWO

WHEN TO WORK FOR FREE

"When you're hunting for a job, money is not the important thing. The important thing is finding something that you like and that you'll enjoy doing all your life. If you're having a hard time getting your dream job, then go to the boss and volunteer to work for nothing for six months. That way, he doesn't risk anything, and you get a chance to show him your stuff."

—MILLER QUARLES, 83, PRESIDENT OF THE CURING OLD-AGE
DISEASE SOCIETY, GEOPHYSICIST, AND FATHER TO THREE

MAKING DECISIONS

"He who hesitates is bossed."

—ROD STEIGER, 73, OSCAR-WINNING ACTOR
AND FATHER TO ONE

THE DIFFERENCE BETWEEN WORK AND A JOB

"The challenge of work is for it to remain a challenge. When work degenerates into a tedious routine, then it is no longer work but only a job. The goal is to maintain your creativity, to articulate your individual character, and to find meaning and fulfillment in your work. That is the difference between work and a job, a calling and a box on an institutional flowchart."

—RABBI BYRON SHERWIN, PH.D., 52, EDUCATOR, AUTHOR OF *WHY BE GOOD?*, AND FATHER TO ONE

THE STUPIDEST THING IN THE WORLD

"Use money to buy what you need, but never use it to buy position, friends, or love. After you buy the necessities, have fun with it. Never let it upset you. That's the stupidest thing in the world. Money has never been important to me. I never had much, rarely had any extra, but I always had enough."

—FRANK EINTERZ, 70, RETIRED VICE-PRESIDENT OF A FOOD-PROCESSING PLANT AND FATHER TO 13

THE CONTRACT

"When it comes to work, I have a very simple premise: If a man is paying you, work for him. When you no longer want to work for him, leave. That's all. It's that simple. Don't stay there and bitch about what you're doing."

—RALPH HAAS, 63, RETIRED RADIO DISC JOCKEY, AUTHOR, AND FATHER TO TWO

CHANCE VS. RISK

"Take chances in your work. Every time I took a chance and made a change, it worked out for the better. There's a difference between taking a chance and taking a risk, though. Chances are calculated."

—GORDY SHIELDS, 80, RETIRED HIGH SCHOOL TEACHER AND COLLEGE COUNSELOR, COMPETITIVE CYCLIST, AND FATHER TO THREE

Changing Jobs

"America used to be the land of lifetime employment, and we never thought about changing careers. But that's not the case anymore. That still doesn't make it routine, though. The day I decided to leave teaching and take a job as a magazine editor, I was all excited. I thought, this is going to be great. But then I went back to my school, and I had the most profound physical reaction I've ever had. I thought I was going to be sick. It was an emotional reaction to turning my back on something that I'd done for 27 years. It was scary heading out into the unknown. But it's really important to do that. I think you should change jobs every 5 to 7 years to get out of those ruts you get in. You have to find a way to renew yourself."
—Fred Matheny, 53, writer, former English teacher, and father to one

How to Become a Big Man

"Do the things your father was afraid to do, the things that he would have considered dangerously feminine: cry, hug your male friends, change diapers, read a romance novel, do the dishes, knit a sweater—whatever it was that he was afraid to do because he was holding tightly to his more rigidly patriarchal, dehumanizing model of masculinity. When you do something that he considered women's stuff, you set yourself free without giving up one drop of testosterone, one Y chromosome."
—Frank Pittman III, M.D., 62, psychiatrist, author of Grow Up!, and father to three

Building Your Reputation

"The best success anyone can have is a good reputation. You develop one by being honest, frank, and accommodating and by practicing understanding. Instead of watching the other fellow with a sense of fear, try to help."
—Joseph McFadden (1922–1997), diplomat, professor of journalism, and father to five

From My Father's Journal

"Restlessness is discontent—and discontent is the first necessity of progress. Show me a thoroughly satisfied man and I will show you a failure."
—Thomas A. Edison

❧

"The purpose of managment is not to get the most out of men, but to get the best out of them."

❧

"It does not take much strength to do things, but it requires great strength to decide on what to do."

❧

"Success formula: Think up a product that costs a dime, sells for a dollar and is habit-forming."

❧

"Obstacles are those terrifying things we see when we take our eyes off our goal."

❧

"You may be on the right track, but you'll get run over if you just stand there."

❧

"It's good to have money and the things that money can buy, but it's good to check once in a while and make sure you haven't lost the things that money can't buy."
—George Horace Lorimer

HOW TO ACQUIRE WISDOM

"The great thinkers begin by knowing what others think. Wisdom comes *after* information and knowledge. And books provide the scaffolding that allows us to build our own system of thought."

—GEORGE SHEEHAN, M.D. (1918–1993), AUTHOR, RUNNER,
PHILOSOPHER, AND FATHER TO 12

BEING A LEADER

"You've got to have integrity, and that comes from being true to yourself. You have to act exactly the way you are. You can't be one person at home and another person at the office. You can't act one way in church on Sunday and a different way at work on Monday. Integrity is when your insides match your outside, when your heart and your feelings match your actions."

—JOE SCIORTINO, 66, RETIRED EXECUTIVE AND FATHER TO TWO

FEED THE BRAIN

"The more you put into your mind, the more valuable you will be to the world. You have a tremendous brain that's far more complicated than any computer man can make. In fact, I think the brain is our soul. The more you put into it, the happier you'll be. The more you use it, the more successful you'll be."

—MILLER QUARLES, 83, PRESIDENT OF THE CURING OLD-AGE
DISEASE SOCIETY, GEOPHYSICIST, AND FATHER TO THREE

GIVING IT A FEW EXTRA MINUTES

"Always take the extra time to do your best, because no one can tell how long you took to do something, but they can always determine the quality of the effort."

—KONRAD SCHEID, 71, RETIRED FACTORY WORKER
AND FATHER TO TWO

SMOKESCREEN INTELLIGENCE

"There's so much stuff to know these days that you really can fool most of the people most of the time. Learn one thing so well that people will assume you must know about other things, too. And if you communicate your one thing with the conviction of a wise man, the chances are that more people will think that you're wise than dumb."
—DENIS BOYLES, 52, PROFESSOR, WRITER, FARMER,
AND FATHER TO THREE

AN EXPERIMENT

"Money costs too much. Put some money in a bowl and set it on fire. Keep doing this until you realize that heat and light are worth more than money. So is your life."
—FRANK PITTMAN III, M.D., 62, PSYCHIATRIST, AUTHOR
OF *GROW UP!*, AND FATHER TO THREE

WORKING YOUR WAY TO THE TOP

"It's like trying to eat an elephant. You have to do it a bite at a time. Or like climbing a mountain. It's one step at a time. I mean, you can't do it all at once. You prepare yourself first with a good education. Then you set a goal. That's important. You have to have a point up there on the wall. You have to say, 'Hey, that's where I want to be.' And you keep your eye on that target."
—BILL BELL, 75, RETIRED MARKETING EXECUTIVE
AND FATHER TO THREE

JOB EXPERIENCE

"Never take a job for which you're eminently qualified. What you know is not nearly as important as what you can learn."
—JERRY SANDS, 61, PROJECT MANAGER AND FATHER TO FOUR

Nervousness

"Anxiety is a good sign. If you're not nervous, then you're not taking enough chances and, ultimately, you won't do well."
—Bob McCoy, 71, curator of the Museum of Questionable Medical Devices and father to three

Pick the Brains of the Best

"Nobody starts out knowing everything. You have to start at the bottom and pick people's brains. When I got out of the service, I became a sheet-metal worker. I was an apprentice for five years. I found out who the top people were in my trade, and I asked to work with them. I asked them a lot of questions. How can we do this a little faster, a little cheaper, a little better? Once they know where you're coming from, they open up."
—Lorenzo Gaytán, 50, Vietnam veteran, sheet-metal worker, post office employee, and father to two

Setting an Example

"The days of giving orders arbitrarily and expecting them to be faithfully carried out are gone. Never ask anybody to do anything that you're not willing to do. From a leadership standpoint, I don't think that you can ask people to stand out in the rain if you're not willing to stand out in the rain. As a matter of fact, you ought to go out and stand in the rain first."
—B. G. Stephens, Ph.D., 63, college administrator, chemist, and father to four

DISCOVERING WHY YOU'RE HERE

"If there's anything that science has told us over the past 300 or 400 years, it's that the universe is a pretty good mechanism. So it isn't a question of discovering the reason we're here as much as it is a question of constructing a reason. I don't think there's necessarily some Supreme Being who's running people off an assembly line and, in my case, says, 'Here comes a Matheny. He's born to teach.' I think you discover what you're born to do, and then you make that your reason for existence.

"So it's a search. Take Michael Jordan, for example. Have him born in 1810. The thing he was born to do did not exist. There he is, with this enormous talent and no field upon which to play. And so maybe people think they don't have a talent or aren't extremely talented, when they are, and the field just doesn't exist. Sometimes you have to make one."
—FRED MATHENY, 53, WRITER, FORMER ENGLISH TEACHER, AND FATHER TO ONE

BECOME AN EXPERT AT SOMETHING

"Master something, anything, no matter how small. It'll give you a tremendous sense of satisfaction and confidence. When I picked up the first book I wrote after it was bound, the tears came. It was like picking up my first child. I finally realized at that minute that I had done something. Up to that point, it was all pieces of paper. I never envisioned what it would look like until the publisher sent it to me with its beautiful blue hardbound cover and gold leaf. I picked it up and realized that I had finally mastered what I had set out to do."
—RALPH HAAS, 63, RETIRED RADIO DISC JOCKEY, AUTHOR, AND FATHER TO TWO

WHO TO DO BUSINESS WITH

"Being a real man has nothing to do with physical strength. It has to do with character. My grandpa once gave me some good advice about that. There was a man he wouldn't do business with, and I asked him why. He said, 'Well, I just don't like the way he takes care of his stock.' He said if you want to know how good a man is, look at his stock. If his cattle, his horses, or nowadays, I guess, his employees or his family, are poorly taken care of, then don't have anything to do with him. This guy is not an honorable person. If he won't take care of them, he won't pay you."

—JIM GORDON, 61, VIETNAM VETERAN, NURSE, SUBSTANCE ABUSE COUNSELOR, AND FATHER TO THREE

ONE SIMPLE TRUTH

"If you break your word, you're no longer a man. Once you break your word, you can't be trusted to keep any contract."

—RALPH HAAS, 63, RETIRED RADIO DISC JOCKEY, AUTHOR, AND FATHER TO TWO

MAJOR IN ADAPTABILITY

"Career. When you're 6 years old, you want to be a fireman. By the time you're 16, you've switched to being a U.S. Marine. When you're 23, it's a teacher's job you want. When you're 30, you wish you had become a preacher. When you're 50, you decide to write your first book. So when you go to college and hear about career opportunities, remember that nothing is forever. What you are and what you want to be is changing all the time. Rather than having one career, it's better to have adaptability."

—THOMAS KEMP, 53, RETIRED CORPORATE MANAGER, VIETNAM VETERAN, AUTHOR, AND FATHER TO THREE

From My Father's Journal

"Many men can rise to the occasion, but few know when to sit down." —J. FIELDS

❦

"Small deeds done are better than large deeds planned."

❦

"Men who talk like big wheels usually are mere spokesmen."

❦

"An expert is a man who knows just that much more about his subject than his associates. Most of us are nearer to the top than we think. We fail to realize how easy it is, how necessary it is to learn that fraction more."

❦

"Nearly every great discovery in science has come as the result of providing a new question rather than a new answer."

❦

"The firefly only shines when on the wing. So it is with man; when once we rest, we darken."

❦

"He who establishes his argument by noise and command, shows that his reason is weak."
—MONTAIGNE

The Boy Scout Code

"As a guideline to your life, follow the Boy Scout Law: 'A scout is trustworthy, loyal, helpful, friendly, courteous, kind, obedient, cheerful, thrifty, brave, clean, and reverent.' That's it. That's all you need to have a successful life."
—Richard Lawrence, 71, ceramic engineer
and father to four (including three Eagle Scouts)

How to Avoid Work Entirely

"For your career, choose something you love to do, and you'll never have to work again."
—Vince Sperrazza, 52, technician and father to four

A Final Test for Success

"How do you gauge success? Well, let me put it this way. If your son or daughter thinks you're successful, then you are."
—John Heiser, M.D., 66, physician, clinical professor
of anesthesia, and father to five

John D. Cahill, 75

John D. Cahill of Salt Lake City spent most of his life building a law practice in Milwaukee, then walked away from the money and the tedium to study Spanish literature and become a hotelier. Now he travels between hotel properties in Colorado, Utah, Wyoming, Montana, Mexico, and Hawaii, climbs mountains such as Kilimanjaro, McKinley, and Aconcagua, and is obsessed with breaking three hours in a marathon. Perhaps most rewarding, many of Cahill's nine children run, climb, and work with him.

WORK: "Do work that you enjoy, and keep looking until you find it. If you want to be a U.S. park ranger and they won't hire you, take a job that will help you get there, then take the next closest job, and keep pounding on that door. Once you get it, give that job everything you have. Then quit when you've had enough and find another job."

SATISFACTION: "If you're happy, if you feel good about what you're doing, then tell the rest of the world to go to hell. Don't let society pressure you."

CHANGING LOVE'S LOCALES: "For me, sex keeps getting better. But you have to keep it exciting—cars, bushes, wherever you can do it."

HEALTH: "You don't wake up at age 55 with a trashed heart. You start trashing it with pizza and cheeseburgers at age 20. Begin a health regimen as early as you can."

FATHERHOOD: "Don't try to make your children into what you want them to be or what you weren't. Educate them, most of all. Make education available to them as long as they want it, anyway they want it."

FRIENDSHIP: "If you want to find out how many friends you have, be prepared for disappointment. To think that you have 10 or 15 real friends is bull. It's more likely that you have 10 or 15 very close *acquaintances*. My definition of a friend is somebody you can call up and say, 'Look, I need $10,000, but I don't know when I'll pay it back and I can't tell you what I need it for.' And

he sends it. Two people have done this for me, only it was $25,000. If you have one or two real friends in life, you're lucky."

REGRETS: "That I'll die before I see what happens to the world in the next 50 years. I'm fascinated with the speed at which technology advances, and I can't imagine what the world will be like in 2050. My regret is my inability to satisfy my curiosity."

LIFE'S MOST UNDERRATED VIRTUE: "Personal integrity. People don't care enough about their own personal integrity. If you say that you'll be somewhere at 10 o'clock and you can't make it, then call and say you're not coming. Cancel reservations at restaurants. Be honest."

Tommy Van Scoy, 78

He never went to college, but he has a Ph.D. in shrewdness. He is a diamond in the rough—a multi-millionaire gem salesman who is equal parts carnival barker, carpetbagger, and, to use his own words, "humanitarian crusader." He is boastful, belligerent, and brassy. He is, in many respects, the personification of the American dream—a Depression kid, an ex-amateur boxer, from the coal regions of Pennsylvania who used his wits to make it big.

Now he drives a Cadillac and smokes fat cigars while overseeing a 14-karat kingdom of Van Scoy Diamond Mine stores along the East Coast. There are many who dislike him, but just as many envy his success, including the eight children he has fathered.

BEING A DREAMER: "Albert Einstein said, 'Imagination is more powerful than knowledge.' If you cannot even imagine yourself as a winner, you will never win."

OPPORTUNITY: "Be alert for anything that you hate doing. No doubt others dislike it, too, so if you can find a way to make the job easier, people will pay out for it."

THE SECRET OF SUCCESS: "Persistence, pushing on, never quitting is the quality in a person that makes the difference between success and failure. Genius alone will not do it. Education alone will not do it. Talent alone will not do it. But persistence will."

WINNING A FIGHT: "I've heard it said, 'Never underestimate your opponent.' However, I've always found that in order to lead a self-confident and fear-free life, it is far better never to *overrate* your opponent."

THE KEY TO HAPPINESS: "The greatest happiness is found striving, hoping, planning, trying, and dreaming of success in some venture, whether it's building a home, a business, a family, or a relationship. That is why you must keep moving your goals higher. It keeps life exciting. When you're no longer striving and there's little left in life but boredom, your health is affected and your death is hastened."

FEARLESSNESS: "Courage is simply the conviction that you're capable of coping with the task at hand. Preparedness is the antidote to fear."

MAKING THE RIGHT DECISION: "Everything that you do has an effect on some other person's life. If you win, someone else has to lose. Therefore, before you ever make a decision to do something, think about how it is going to affect everyone else in your world and discuss it with them. Hear and try to understand their opinions. It will help you make a wiser decision."

LEADERSHIP: "Man was never meant to be a follower. Remember, just because everyone seems to be doing something in a certain way doesn't mean that it's the best way. Be a maverick."

LUCK: "The harder I work, the luckier I get."

Chapter 3

God

My father knelt and prayed every night beside his bed. Sometimes, as I walked the narrow hall to my own room, I'd see him there in his white Jockeys and T-shirt, head bowed, lamp dimmed, and hands clasped. As a child, I was not proud of this. When you're a boy, and you see your father alone on his knees, it's disappointing. He's done wrong, he needs help, he's weak.

I used to tell my best friends all our family secrets—that my parents argued violently, that my dad was often drunk, even that my uncle was a crazy bum who lived by the river in a shack, but I never told them that my father kneeled. That seemed too personal, too much an embarrassing part of my future inheritance.

To this day, I don't know what my father was praying for so fervently (although I suspect it was me). Nor do I understand what convinced him that his bed was just as powerful as a pew. He never offered an explanation, and I never asked for one. In time, it grew to bother me less and became just another quirky old-man's habit.

In the meantime, I endured 12 years of Catholic school, including time on the front line as an altar boy. I heard every gospel, memorized every commandment, and mechanically celebrated each Holy Day. Until I was old enough to exert my free will, I went to church every Sunday. We stood there, my father and me, he with his rosary and I with a thousand other threads of unrelated thought.

Now that I'm grown, I rarely go to church anymore. I find that it makes me angry. My wife convinced me to send our children to the Catholic equivalent of Sunday school. But instead of them arriving home cherubic with newfound knowledge, they shrug indifferently at the experience and hand me boxes of kid-size envelopes they're given so that they can make donations, too.

Nevertheless, I consider myself a religious man. I believe in God, and that there are pieces of him, called love and goodness, in everyone. I also believe in prayer, not the memorized type mumbled in church but the spontaneous kind spoken, ironically, in the last breath of the day, when the lamp has been dimmed and the bedspread drawn down, and it's just you and those pieces of God in you, alone.

Sometimes I find it hard to believe that the thing I remember best from all that religious indoctrination, the lesson that penetrated my rebellious attitude the most and succeeded in making me religious, was the simple sight of my father on his knees beside his bed each night. That was all it took. That was the seed of my soul.

So I do the same thing now, in my underwear no less, because I find that it keeps me humble and prompts thankfulness. I suspect that when a man grows too big to kneel, then he is destined to fall.

I do it, too, because that's when I feel closest to my dad. He is there with me while I pray. In fact, he *is* me, one of those pieces of love and goodness that I call God. If I didn't do this, I would lose touch, not only with him but also myself.

And, above all, I do it for my children, with the hope that as they walk back to their rooms through our narrow hall, they'll notice me. And while at first they may think there's something wrong, that I need help, that I'm weak, I know eventually that they'll come to realize it's because I wanted to do more, that I welcomed help, and that I was far from meek.

The Proof Is in the Perfection

"The other morning I went hunting. It was so nice by the river. There were wood duck, beaver, and lots of squirrels playing. It was so beautiful, I didn't even shoot anything. I just sat there drinking my coffee and enjoying it. If you get outdoors and really spend some time there, it's hard not to believe in God. It's hard to say that all this just came to pass. I mean, look at the perfection. Look at the beauty! Things like that don't just happen."

—Jim Gordon, 61, Vietnam veteran, nurse, substance abuse counselor, and father to three

Fear God Less, Trust Yourself More

"Too much of religion is based on fear—the fear of the unknown, the fear of God's wrath. That approach never made sense to me. I always felt that I should answer to my own conscience and the consciences of people around me rather than to some Higher Power. Accept yourself first of all. You are a living, breathing being, the result of billions of years of evolution. Be proud of that. I'm not really concerned about what happens when I die. Other than a great sense of curiosity, I don't care."

—Gordy Shields, 80, retired high school teacher and college counselor, competitive cyclist, and father to three

The Big Picture

"Unless you have something beyond yourself that's more important, more significant, more in control of your life, then you're going to have a very narrow view of life."

—Alfred Williams, 64, former president county judge, survivor of two heart operations, and father to three

WHAT REMAINS AFTER ALL IS LOST

"When you think you've lost everything, you still have God. On the very same day, I lost a part-time job on which I depended, and my eldest daughter was picked up for shoplifting. My wife had already left me, saying I was worthless. It was all very traumatic. I didn't know what I was going to do. Then, for some reason, I recalled the Book of Job, which I had studied in Bible school, and how Job had lost everything, except God. I realized that was true for me, too. God is there. God is all I've got. And that very day, I went to a Pentecostal church meeting, confessed that I'd gone astray, and asked God to come into my life in a fuller way. Right there, I was filled with a sudden peace, and I realized that I really was somebody. I am a child of God."
—DON RANNEY, M.D., 67, PROFESSOR EMERITUS OF ANATOMY AND KINESIOLOGY AND FATHER TO FOUR

ATTAINING BLISS

"Don't depend on God to make you happy. You have to do that yourself."
—MILLER QUARLES, 83, PRESIDENT OF THE CURING OLD-AGE DISEASE SOCIETY, GEOPHYSICIST, AND FATHER TO THREE

SKEPTICS ARE NOT ATHEISTS

"What worries me is that young people are often taught that there's a great absolute truth and knowledge out there. So when somebody comes along and convinces them that they have it, off they go. That's why cults are so prevalent. My advice is to develop your own view through learning and contemplation because no one knows for sure the nature and intent of God, and you have to be skeptical of those who claim they do. That's not atheism. That's not agnosticism. It's just healthy skepticism."
—B. G. STEPHENS, PH.D., 63, COLLEGE ADMINISTRATOR, CHEMIST, AND FATHER TO FOUR

IN SEARCH OF A SATISFYING LIFE

"To me, there is no valid metaphysical knowledge to support the existence of God. So if there is a God, to me it's Mother Nature. I don't see any supernatural forces at work in the world. I don't believe in heaven or hell, other than they're here on Earth sometimes. There's just no basis for believing these kinds of things, although it does give comfort to a lot of people. But I learned early through the inspiration of my father to read philosophy—writers such as John Stuart Mill and Bertrand Russell. They gave me the spiritual information I needed by helping me understand what the major questions were in life. I consider myself religious now, but I would define religion as the shared quest for the values of a satisfying life."

—BOB McCOY, 71, CURATOR OF THE MUSEUM
OF QUESTIONABLE MEDICAL DEVICES AND FATHER TO THREE

BEING SAVED

"I don't like telling this story because people think I'm crazy, but I swear it's true. I was dying at 43. I had no job and no money, and my wife had left me because I was a violent alcoholic. Sitting by the river one day, I thought about killing myself. I went back to my room and cried like a baby saying, 'Dear God, if you really exist, help.' Then the radio came on. I still get goose pimples thinking about it. I don't know how it turned on, but there was a minister saying, 'You need God, you need salvation, you are a lost soul.' I started shaking. 'He's talking to me,' I thought. And that was when my whole life started over. The lesson I learned was to never lose hope. Be a believer in something bigger than yourself. Call it God or Allah or Buddha or whatever. Listen to your conscience. That's the voice of God."

—RUDY SANCHEZ, 81, FORMER NIGHTCLUB ENTERTAINER
AND FATHER TO ONE

From My Father's Journal

"Do not pray for gold. Pray for good children, happy grandchildren." —CHINESE PROVERB

❧

"God is with those who persevere." —THE KORAN

❧

"The best way to know God is to love many things." —VINCENT VAN GOGH

❧

"I have never met a healthy person who worried much about his health, or a good person who worried much about his soul." —JOHN HALDANE

❧

"The most acceptable service of God is doing good to men."

❧

"You have not lived a perfect day, even though you have earned your money, unless you have done something for someone who will never be able to repay you."

❧

"Every charitable act is a stepping stone toward heaven."

❧

"Some people carry their religion on their backs like a burden, when they should carry it like a song in their hearts."

MIRACLES

"About seven years ago, my wife got cancer. She was dying. The doctors told me it was terminal. When I saw science failing, I went to the chapel and prayed. I told God that I'd accept whatever He decided but please try to spare her. I promised to be a better man. And eventually, she got better. Miracles are not easy to identify, but I believe that God had something to do with this. If you can answer all the secrets of nature, you may not need to believe in God. But if you have no explanation for certain things, like why a rose is red, why an ant is still better than any machine ever created by man, or why my wife was saved, then perhaps there is something."
—RICARDO SUAREZ, 56, ATTORNEY, EL SALVADOR
PRESIDENTIAL CANDIDATE, AND FATHER TO THREE

WHERE TO LOOK

"The best advice I ever heard about God came from Albert Einstein. He said, 'I don't believe in a God who concerns himself with the fate and actions of man. I believe in a God who reveals himself in the harmony of everything that exists.' "
—FRED MATHENY, 53, WRITER, FORMER ENGLISH TEACHER,
AND FATHER TO ONE

WHAT HAPPENS ON JUDGMENT DAY

"When you die, God puts a tape measure around your heart to see how much you've loved and served others."
—CHARLES KOVAC, 70, RETIRED CORPORATE VICE-PRESIDENT
AND FATHER TO SEVEN

HE IS BECAUSE HE PERSISTS

"Any legend that can persist for that many thousands of years must have some truth in it. Nobody could pull off a scam like that."
—JIM GORDON, 61, VIETNAM VETERAN, NURSE, SUBSTANCE
ABUSE COUNSELOR, AND FATHER TO THREE

A DIFFERENT REASON TO GO TO CHURCH

"Going to church can actually make you healthier. Study after study has shown that the happiness and contentment engendered by faith is an extraordinary contributor to overall health. Worship services are full of potentially therapeutic elements—music, aesthetic surroundings, familiar rituals, prayer and contemplation, distraction from everyday tensions, the opportunity for socializing and friendship, and education. Religious people consistently report greater life satisfaction, marital satisfaction, well-being, altruism, and self-esteem than do nonreligious people."
—HERBERT BENSON, M.D., 63, PRESIDENT OF A MIND/BODY
MEDICAL INSTITUTE, AUTHOR OF *TIMELESS HEALING*,
AND FATHER TO TWO

THE LOCATION OF HEAVEN AND HELL

"I'm no theologian and have no plans to become one, but maybe, just maybe, the reality of heaven and hell lies within each one of us; that the seat of the soul, sought for centuries, is actually the unconscious mind; and that it is the unconscious mind that exists for eternity. We, therefore, live forever with the knowledge of the good or ill that we have done. Hence, we carry our own individual heavens and hells within us."
—PETER SWET, 55, WRITER WHO SURVIVED A STROKE
AT AGE 49, AND FATHER TO TWO

SPIRITUALITY VS. RELIGION

"Spirituality and religion are not the same thing. Religion is man's attempt to control things. Spirituality is your own basic belief that there's a higher being who had a hand in building this world. Keep that difference in mind."
—JIM GORDON, 61, VIETNAM VETERAN, NURSE, SUBSTANCE
ABUSE COUNSELOR, AND FATHER TO THREE

Private Worship

"I go to church every Sunday morning, but I don't do it the conventional way. Instead, I go for a bike ride through the beautiful rolling farmland here in southeastern Pennsylvania. I look at the scenery. I wave at the people I pass. And I'm thankful for what God has given me. I learned long ago that you don't need to be inside a church to be religious. I view the entire world as my church and those few precious hours outdoors each Sunday morning as my holy communion."

—Arthur Berger, 63, business executive and father to three

Pumping Spiritual Iron

"Be a little spiritual every day. Make it a discipline. I say morning and evening prayers using a book called *The Daily Office*. Every month, it takes me through all 150 Psalms and, over the course of a year, through a complete reading of Holy Scripture. Regular prayer helps me see patterns and gives me a depth of understanding and insight. Faith opens your eyes to knowledge. Think of it as pumping spiritual iron. If you give up, then you get flabby. You don't have to do it this way, though. The Buddhists meditate. Some people read great books. The point is just to be a little spiritual, a little contemplative, every day. If you do, then over time, your understanding will deepen, religion will become more meaningful, and your faith will become real."

—Derald W. Stump, Ph.D., 67, Episcopalian minister, marital and family therapist, and father to three

How to Talk to the Almighty

"There is one master builder who put this universe together. And you can talk to him directly. You don't need any middleman for that."

—H. T. Bremer, 64, construction engineer and father to four

WHY GOD IS GOOD FOR YOUR HEALTH

"Religious faith is a very important element of good health. After giving a concern or a worry your best effort, analysis, and resolution, it allows you to leave it behind, to put it in God's hands. Someone once said, 'Write your worries in the sand.' I spend my winters by the beach, and I do a lot of that."

—ALFRED WILLIAMS, 64, FORMER PRESIDENT COUNTY JUDGE, SURVIVOR OF TWO HEART OPERATIONS, AND FATHER TO THREE

YOUR BODY OF EVIDENCE

"To find God, learn to doubt doubt. There is so much evidence that behind the universe there is a mind. Consider the complexity of your own eyes. Light falls on the retinas, reflecting images that are transmitted to the brain, which in turn creates meaning. It's just awfully hard for me to believe that this mechanism came about through accident. There must be some great designer of the universe, the world, and the human person. Faith comes from simple observations like this. There are ducks and there are ponds. There are boys, and there are girls. Our needs have been provided for. There's a symmetry to the world that couldn't have resulted from chance. It would be like a newspaper resulting from an explosion at a printing factory."

—DERALD W. STUMP, PH.D., 67, EPISCOPALIAN MINISTER, MARITAL AND FAMILY THERAPIST, AND FATHER TO THREE

MAKING RELIGION STICK

"Unless you make a public commitment, religion won't stick. You can't be a secret believer, a secret Christian. It's like if someone puts a big steak in front of you, done exactly the way you like it. You can smell it, you can look at it, but it's not going to do your body and soul any good until you put your knife into it, cut it, and eat it."

—HENRY IKEMOTO, 74, RETIRED PROBATION OFFICER AND FATHER TO FOUR

From My Father's Journal

"When everything is leaving you, leave everything to God."

⚜

"We have come from somewhere and are going somewhere. The Great Architect of the Universe never built a stairway that leads nowhere."

⚜

"Who falls for love of God, shall rise a star."

⚜

"The first virtue is to restrain the tongue; he approaches nearest to God who knows how to be silent, even though he is in the right."

⚜

"The saint never has to appear holy, but the hypocrite does."

⚜

"Service is the rent that we pay for our room on Earth."

⚜

"At my judgement I should like God to say, I have heard my Mother speak of you."

⚜

"The world has forgotten, in its concern with Left and Right, that there is an Above and Below."

MOST PREACHERS ARE DEAF

"People who want to share their religious views with you almost never want you to share yours with them."
—ROLAND BYRE, 71, GUN SHOP OWNER AND FATHER TO TWO

THE BEST LIFE INSURANCE

"Religious faith doesn't protect you from having bad things happen; it gives you the strength to survive them once they do happen."
—GENE KRZYWINSKI, 43, ELECTRONICS SPECIALIST, HEART ATTACK SURVIVOR, AND FATHER TO TWO

ACTS OF GOD

"In 1972, Hurricane Agnes swept through the Wyoming Valley of Pennsylvania. My home was flooded, and my seven children and pregnant wife had to flee in the middle of the night. I tried to save what I could, but I got trapped by the rising water. A helicopter eventually rescued me from the roof. It would have been easy to blame God for doing this to us, but I don't believe in acts of God, only acts of nature. Men who blame God for their misfortune aren't strong enough to handle misfortune themselves."
—JOHN OSTROWSKI, 70, RETIRED GARMENT CUTTER AND FATHER TO EIGHT

THE ONE TRUE PURPOSE OF RELIGION

"Undoubtedly, the greatest function of religion is to re-mind ourselves that we are not God."
—FRANK PITTMAN III, M.D., 62, PSYCHIATRIST, AUTHOR OF GROW UP!, AND FATHER TO THREE

David Allen, 68

David Allen is dying. His 68-year-old body, weary from the cancer that riddles it, creaks like the old porch swing he loves to sit upon outside his North Carolina home—the one flying the big American flag. He rocks not in despair for a life too quickly gone, but rather in contentment at the small difference that he has managed to make. This simple, unassuming dry cleaner, who dropped out of school in the ninth grade, estimates that he has donated a half-million dollars to charity, funded the construction of 20 churches, and shipped 20,000 Bibles worldwide. All the advertisements, bills, and coupons for his business carry patriotic messages or scripture quotes—a quiet campaign for world betterment that he calls silent evangelism. Although Allen has lost a father to desertion, a wife to cancer, and one of his four children to suicide, he doesn't really feel like he has lost anything. In fact, he's apparently found what we're all searching for.

CONTENTMENT: "If you live a life of usefulness, trying always to help others, then you need not seek happiness. It'll come with each rising sun. And there's really, I found, no better exercise for the heart than reaching down and picking someone else up. Because when you help someone else, you help yourself. Those who bring sunshine to others cannot keep it from themselves."

SERVICE: "Our society doesn't like this word. Very few people today ever experience the real joy of serving others. You know, if you take s-e-r-v out of the word service, all you're left with is i-c-e."

FINDING GOD: "You have to show him some respect. In other words, going to church is the first thing I would recommend. If you don't feel good about the church you're in, scout around and find one that feels like it's your place. Then read the Bible a little bit each day, pray to God, and always be thankful for what he has given you. As a result, somewhere along the line, you're going to feel a little nudge from God, that you're saved. You just can't get saved anytime you want. You have to feel that nudge.

"I used to be a half-hearted Christian. I'd go to church only when I felt like it. Then, one Sunday afternoon, I was out driving, trying to find some good music on the radio, when I flipped on Billy Graham. I didn't know who it was. But his preaching was so dynamic, so edifying, it caught my attention, and I felt the Lord."

LOSING SOMEONE YOU LOVE: "That's hard for a lot of people to understand, and I think that some get bitter at God because of it. My first wife was only 53 when she died, and my son was 41 when he killed himself. But the Bible says that it's appointed unto a man when to die. So I try to remember that God's way is not our way. His ways are higher than our ways. Of course, I grieved. But there's nothing you can do about it, so I just accept the fact that it was their time and I resolved to relive their good memories and make the best of it."

BIGGEST REGRET: "Dropping out of school. Even though I've done a lot of studying to educate myself, it has given me a terrible inferiority complex. People tell me that I don't need to feel that way, that I'm successful, but I just can't help it. It never leaves me."

BEING A SUCCESSFUL BUSINESSMAN: "The secret is having a good relationship with your customers and employees alike. Most people realize that about the customer, but the employees are just as important. I try to create a bond between me and my employees. Every morning, I speak to each one, ask about their loved ones, get to know them. When they're having personal problems, I try to help out, even loan them money, if necessary. I try to promote good relationships because they're doing me a favor by working, just like I'm doing them a favor by supplying jobs. So it goes hand in hand. And those who work extra hard, I reward with a bonus of verbal praise. You'd be surprised how much a compliment or caring attitude means to a person's attitude."

RESTARTING A STALLED SOUL: "People are like old automobiles. Sometimes they start, and sometimes they need some help. I've had plenty of people give me a push when I was stalled. And I've pushed a lot of people, too. A little push is all they need to get going and be self-sufficient again."

WHEN YOUR DAUGHTER BRINGS HOME A BOY: "Teach her how to choose a man of integrity for a life partner. Beginning when she's a little girl, show her how to look for quality in people. I told all mine, when you have a boyfriend and you're considering getting serious, check his work record. There are some boys that just won't work. And if he's a job hopper or if he has no ambition, then steer clear."

THE END: "They took out my left kidney. I got a big old tumor in my right shoulder and two hot spots in my right thigh that they're giving me radiation for. I use a crutch to get around. Sometimes things hurt pretty bad. But I'm just thankful that things aren't worse. I could be bedridden or in a wheelchair. You've got to look up and see the stars, because if you look down, all you see is mud."

Tom Cannon, 72

His two sons will probably be surprised to see him in this book, surrounded by all these model fathers. By his own admission, he is not close to either one, and when he talks of his disabled wife of 51 years, his tone seems more laden with tolerance than love. Tom Cannon is an outcast in his hometown of Richmond, Virginia. He is misunderstood and alone, living in a beat-up neighborhood on a retired postal-clerk salary of $16,800 per year. But Cannon is perhaps the richest and wisest father featured here. During the past 25 years, he has given away approximately $100,000 (usually in $1,000 increments) to people he hardly knows—people whose only connection to him is that they are human and that they, too, are forgotten and in need.

Could there be any better example set by a father?

HELPING OTHERS: "I view myself as a composite, at least in consciousness, of all the people who have impacted my life and helped me develop into the being I am today. I feel a oneness with the rest of humanity. And that's not just talk, it's fact. So when I'm helping other humans, it's equivalent to helping myself because I am a part of them and they are a part of me. We all have an obligation to help as we have been helped."

AFFORDING THE UNAFFORDABLE: "People always ask me how I can afford to give away money. It's simple. I don't have any big expensive vices to support. I don't do drugs, I don't smoke, I don't gamble, and I don't chase after women."

WHEN TO SPEAK UP: "Nobody likes to brag, and people should be humble, but only to a point. I'm not a status seeker. I'm not asking anybody to vote for me. I never solicited publicity, but I feel that I have a message to deliver, and I wouldn't get it across if I were secretive about what I'm doing. Our children need more examples of good deeds and acts of love. The evil that man does is shouted from the rooftops daily. It's ridiculous to be humble about the good things you do and keep them out of sight as if they were something to be ashamed of."

MONEY: "People are infinitely more important than money. That's why I give mine away."

RELIGION: "It may surprise you to learn that I don't belong to any church. I don't answer to any man-made theological system. What counts is your behavior, not what you believe or what somebody taught you to believe. If you worship in a certain faith and don't live that faith, then it has no meaning."

HEAVEN: "It doesn't appeal to me. The concept of some kind of gold-plated welfare state up in the sky where people loll around for eternity on their ethereal asses plucking harps is not for me. I don't want the paradise of some other world. I want to go on learning, growing, and serving in this world."

FATHERHOOD: "I'm not close to either of my sons because I was kind of strict with them growing up. What I was trying to do was what any good father would try to do: keep them from self-destructing on drugs and violence. We lived in a slum-type area, and I never permitted them to roam the streets. And, of course, they chafed at that kind of restriction and discipline. But I believed, and still believe, in hard love. You don't have to worry about your kids loving you if you're keeping them from self-destructing. If you let them go out and wreck their lives, they'll only blame you later for not being stricter."

THE MEANING OF LIFE: "We hear a lot about being happy. We're supposed to have that as our goal. But one man's happiness may be another man's sorrow. I think the greatest thing that we are here to do is grow. And some of our greatest growth and wisdom stems from misery, unhappiness, pain, and suffering. Now if we can do the things that give us great growth and find happiness at the same time, then that's ideal. But happiness in itself ought not to be the primary objective of life."

Chapter 4

Sex, Women, and Love

My father never said the word *sex* to me. He never told a raunchy joke in my presence. And he never had me pause in suspended brotherly awe to watch a truly beautiful woman float by. If the female body is a museum of fine art, then that's one place my father and I never spent a Saturday.

He caught me once. I was in the basement with the Sunday Sears, Roebuck flyer, erasing the underwear off women in the advertisements. I was 13 at the time and had learned this graphic technique from a kid in eighth grade named Mitch. By delicately erasing the bra and panties from a woman in a black-and-white ad, and then artfully penciling in what was supposed to be underneath, you could manufacture some pretty convincing do-it-yourself pornography.

I had gotten so enthralled in my work, immersed in a true sweet spot in time, that I didn't hear him come down the steps or notice that he was looking over my shoulder. When he asked, "What are you doing?" I almost shot through the ceiling. I think I said, "Drawing stuff," but I couldn't clear things away fast enough to support that generalization.

All he said as he swiped the pictures into a wastebasket was, "I'm disappointed in you." Then he walked back up the steps and never mentioned it again. There was no punishment, no explanation of procreation, just that. At the time, I was relieved. But before long, I started wondering exactly how I had let him down. What did he expect from me?

Another time, a few years later, we were on a fishing trip in New Brunswick, Canada, just my father and I in a small cabin in the wilderness with nothing to do all day but float, cast, and hope. The family that owned the nearby lodge had a daughter about my age who helped her grandmother serve the evening meal and clean the guest cabins. She was pretty. She was friendly. And, naturally, after spending summers alone in the woods, she was very interested in me.

Despite that episode with the Sears flyer, I was still more entranced with fishing than with girls at this point in my puberty. So I didn't immediately notice what was happening. She started hanging around a lot, complimenting us on the day's catch and fussing over our dinner even more than her grandma did. Until one night I found myself alone with her on the dock by the lake.

New Brunswick summer nights are slow to come. It doesn't get dark in this far-eastern province until 10:30 P.M.. But when it does, the stars are like strings of sparkling white Christmas lights strung off the moon. And the cry of the loons echoes across the water, sorrowful and soothing as a saxophone.

It was the type of perfect romantic setting that you strive to construct for special occasions, only we had fallen into it. Just talking and being with her was somehow so nice, I didn't want it to end.

"Joe! Joe, are you down there?"

It was my father, squinting off the porch of our cabin, about a hundred yards up the hill.

"Yeah, yeah I'm here. I'll be up in a few minutes."

She and I brushed aside the interruption and started talking again, so increasingly entranced with each other that even the blackflies, which were ravenous at this hour, couldn't distract us. I had never felt this way about a girl before.

"Joe! It's time to come up. It's late."

My father was insistent now, and I was embarrassed by it. It was obvious that he was more worried about the girl than me, or me with this girl. So I said I had to go, waved a quick good-bye and walked away from her—forever.

When I got back to the cabin, my father asked if I felt like playing cards. "No," I replied, upset at his nonchalance. "Why couldn't I stay by the lake?"

But he just mumbled, "It's getting late," and dealt two hands of 500 rummy. We stayed up and played cards past midnight, until I beat him real bad.

The only association I have of my father with sex was a book that I found in a bureau by his bed. It was Alex Comfort's classic *The Joy of Sex*, complete with pages of explicit illustrations. Whenever he and my mother would leave the house, I would sneak it out and sit in trembling wonder on the hall steps. Then, minutes or hours later, when I heard them at the door, I would put it back, exactly as it had been. He never caught me doing this, but I had caught him, and something about that made me feel better.

I took him to a strip club once. It was a decade later, with buddies at my bachelor party. He tried to be one of the guys, with a bottle of Miller High Life in his hand and a grin on his face, but he was obviously nervous and uncomfortable. Come to think of it, I don't even remember him watching the girls too closely. No hoots. No whistles. He just stood in the background, talking with my uncle, and was among the first to suggest that we leave.

I can see now that I learned much about women and sex from my father. I absorbed his uneasiness when around them, and I acquired his discomfort with honest sexual discussions. I can't totally forgive him for either.

But I also inherited something else, a trait that's increasingly rare nowadays and one that I've grown proud of. He taught me, in his own stumbling, unorthodox, wordless way, to respect women—that they are more than one-night stands and objects of amusement. In every instance, there's a soul beneath that supple, scented skin, and you should never stroke one without first touching the other.

THE OTHER WOMAN

"No matter how much you love your wife, another woman is going to come along and bring something alive in you that you thought was dead or never knew existed. She is going to fascinate you and obsess you and fill you with desire. You are going to want her and it is going to feel natural.

"Whenever I feel a surge of attraction to a woman, I think of my left leg. I broke it several years ago when I slipped on a patch of ice. Unfaithfulness snaps a relationship as surely as that fall snapped my bone. At first, it may seem like nothing. Over time, you may even be able to mend the break so that the relationship is stronger than ever. But it is not healed. The scar remains, and it will haunt you forever."

—KENT NERBURN, PH.D., FROM HIS BOOK
LETTERS TO MY SON

SEX IS OVERRATED

"Men get worried because they hear there's no sex in old age. Well, my first 20 years of life weren't bad, and there was no sex then, either."

—MOE TURNER, 80, RETIRED MILITARY SCIENTIST
AND FATHER TO FIVE

THE LOTTERY OF LOVE

"You have to be awfully lucky to find the right mate. At that time of life, at that young age, very few men are wise enough to make a decision on any logical basis. I don't believe there's any advice worth listening to about this. It just takes an enormous amount of luck."

—GENE COOPER, 83, RETIRED PROFESSOR OF ENGINEERING,
HUSBAND FOR 60 YEARS, AND FATHER TO TWO

The Secret to a Happy Marriage

"You can't all of a sudden have love. Physical attraction isn't love. There has to be something besides that. It may sound corny, but I truly believe that one of the secrets to a happy marriage is having a longer relationship beforehand. That way you develop respect for each other and realize that she's not perfect and neither are you. My wife and I had a five-year relationship before we got married, and there was no sex beforehand. Nowadays, people laugh at that as ridiculous, but we've never had any problems. We *expected* to live together the rest of our lives."

—Charles VanBuskirk (1917–1998), quality control engineer, husband for 55 years, and father to two

How to Drive a Woman Wild

"A good sex life doesn't require a perfect body, and it has nothing to do with the size or shape of any body part. It has to do with your ability and willingness to reach out and touch another human being. Above all, a woman needs to be listened to and respected. When you get into her space and appreciate her for who she is, you'll get a marvelous response."

—Paul Gethard, 65, sex surrogate, handyman, and father to eight

50/50 Isn't Enough

"Marriage is a 60/60 proposition. Always give 10 percent more than you expect."

—Gordy Shields, 80, retired high school teacher and college counselor, husband for 50 years, and father to three

WHAT TO DO WHEN SHE SAYS "NOT TONIGHT"

"Lots of guys who cheat on their wives plead sexual deprivation or boredom at home. And, often enough, a good case can be made. But if your sex life isn't everything you dreamed, make sure that you've given it everything you've got. Ask yourself how much ingenuity, improv, energy, joy, and lust *you* bring to the sheets."

—HUGH O'NEILL, 46, AUTHOR, EDITOR, AND FATHER TO TWO

HOW TO END IT

"If you want to leave the woman you're with, have the courage to do it cleanly. Do not subject her to the destructive cycle that is designed to make your unhappiness appear as her fault. It's not her fault; it's not your fault. It's the way you feel, and you have nothing to be ashamed of."

—RANDY WAYNE WHITE, 48, FISHING GUIDE, WRITER,
AND FATHER TO TWO

THE RISK OF LOVING

"Among the greatest blessings in life is to love and be loved. But that's also hard, because in order to love you have to be vulnerable."

—ALFRED WILLIAMS, 64, FORMER PRESIDENT COUNTY JUDGE
AND FATHER TO THREE

COMPLIMENTING A WOMAN

"'You're beautiful' isn't a compliment. Compliment her on what she has made, not on what God has made. 'Lovely dress,' 'terrific memo,' 'incredible insight,' 'great joke!'"

—DENIS BOYLES, 52, PROFESSOR, WRITER, FARMER,
AND FATHER TO THREE

KEEPING A RELATIONSHIP FRESH

"When you hear of older people who have been married for 40 or 50 years, your first reaction is, 'My God! Where's the excitement? She probably has all her own habits, and he probably has his.' But that's not true. The woman you're married to today is not the same woman you married, and you are not the same man. You're both constantly changing. That person you're making love to today is different from the one you were with even yesterday. If you keep this in mind, having her say yes will make it just as exciting as the first time."

—CHARLES KOVAC, 70, RETIRED CORPORATE VICE-PRESIDENT, HUSBAND FOR 47 YEARS, AND FATHER TO SEVEN

HOW TO GET A DATE WITH A SUPERMODEL

"Two of the main traits that beautiful women are attracted to in men are power and self-confidence. If you're intimidated by a woman's looks, she assumes that you're going to be intimidated by the world in general."

—WARREN FARRELL, PH.D., 55, AUTHOR OF *WHY MEN ARE THE WAY THEY ARE* AND STEPFATHER TO TWO

THE BODY'S VIAGRA

"If you exercise and keep your testosterone level up, you'll be as sexually active at 65 as you were at 35. I guarantee it. I tell all the young guys at the gym this, but they don't believe me. But I know how I feel. You will reap this reward from exercise down the road. It's an absolute."

—HARRY SCOTT, 65, USA MASTERS BODYBUILDING CHAMP AND FATHER TO THREE

Lust

"Cherish your lust. When the guys who wrote the Bible made lust one of the seven deadly sins, they were talking about bad lust, the kind that hoots at and objectifies women. I'm talking about good lust, the kind that might even be described as zest or vitality, maybe reverence, perhaps an appreciation of all God's children. Remember, the feelings are not a problem; acting on them is."
—Hugh O'Neill, 46, author, editor, and father to two

Vitality

"Don't ever let anybody tell you that sex cannot continue almost indefinitely. It can."
—Gene Cooper, 83, retired professor of engineering, husband for 60 years, and father to two

The Best Pickup Line

"There's only one that works: 'Hi.' Introduce yourself, ask her about herself, and then—and this is important—shut up and listen. I've seen countless guys end up alone because they think that impressing a woman means spelling out their life stories. Salesmen call this a shotgun approach: Tell her everything, and maybe she'll find something to like. Trust me, this strategy stinks. Instead of talking about you, talk about her, and once she's talking, don't interrupt. All a woman wants to know is if you're a man who pays attention to what really counts. And that's *her*."
—Denis Boyles, 52, professor, writer, farmer, and father to three

Let Your Spouse Laugh at You

"On the first date my wife and I ever had, I parked my car on her precipitous driveway and went to ring her bell. Only my car started rolling away. When she came to the door, I was single-handedly trying to stop it. I heard her laughing and realized that this woman knows I'm a fool but is still willing to go out with me. Nobody ever made me feel so comfortable so quickly, and I knew I'd marry her. I could be myself here. I think problems arise when people try to act perfect with one another, avoid criticism, and pretend that they never do anything wrong. Everyone needs to be laughed at, to be told when they're full of crap. If you treat your spouse as an equal and grant her this right, then marriage is a wonderfully humbling learning experience."

—Frank Pittman III, M.D., 62, psychiatrist, author of *Grow Up!*, husband for 38 years, and father to three

You're Not the One and Only

"The terms *soulmate* and *spiritual partner* are effective in infomercials thumping psychic hotlines, but they are an illusion in all other respects. Remind yourself that your soulmate found guys to sleep with before she met you, and she'll find guys to sleep with after you're gone."

—Randy Wayne White, 48, fishing guide, writer, and father to two

Keep No Secrets

"There is no such thing as 'none of your business' in an intimate relationship."

—Brad Blanton, Ph.D., 58, clinical psychologist, director of the Center for Radical Honesty, and father to two

From My Father's Journal

"Our faith and our friendships are not shattered by one big act, but by many small neglects."
—J. GUSTAV WHITE

❧

"The love of liberty is the love of others, the love of power is the love of ourselves." —WILLIAM HAZLITT

❧

"To be trusted is a greater compliment than to be loved."

❧

"It requires a long time to become thoroughly acquainted with anyone."

❧

"Nobody's family can hang out the sign, 'Nothing the matter here.'" —CHINESE PROVERB

❧

"When you want to win an argument, you'll be mighty wise to say, 'I can see it from your point of view.'"

❧

"Quarrels would never last long if there were not faults on both sides." —LA ROCHEFOUCAULD

How to Get Her to Do Anything

"The secret for getting my wife to be less inhibited had more to do with me than her. It wasn't until I started listening to what she wanted from me *outside* the bedroom that changes happened *inside* the bedroom. I needed to show that I loved her by talking to her and treating her as my equal in all aspects of life. Once she became secure and felt deeply loved by me, all her inhibitions disappeared. Damn, I wish I had figured that out sooner."

—Danny G., 58, accountant, husband for 24 years, and father to three

Rules of Engagement

"Your fiancée's worst and best behaviors will be magnified during marriage. Expect the things that irritate you now to become annoying and almost distracting. And expect the things that are sweet and loving about her now to become endearing trademarks meant for you alone. If her best doesn't outweigh her worst by a large margin now, then you should reconsider your marriage plans."

—C. David Elm, 63, farmer, husband for 42 years, and father to eight

How to Find the Perfect Mate

"If you're having trouble finding a mate, make a list of all the desirable qualities that you're looking for in a woman. Approach it as if you're hiring someone. List 10 or 15 categories—religious beliefs, type of music, a love of the outdoors—then put an ad in the paper. When I did this, I got 51 replies. I went out with 17 of them, checking off the qualities, plus or minus, that I was looking for. One of them accused me of doing research, which I guess I was, but it worked. My present wife and I have been happily married for 12 years."

—Don Ranney, M.D., 67, professor emeritus of anatomy and kinesiology and father to four

HUGS

"To have a successful marriage, tell your wife you love her every day. If that's difficult for you to do, then give her a hug. Hugs and kisses are very, very inexpensive, but they are very, very good."

—BILL BELL, 75, RETIRED MARKETING EXECUTIVE, HUSBAND FOR 52 YEARS, AND FATHER TO THREE

WHAT YOU'RE MISSING

"A successful marriage is one in which it never occurs to you that you've compromised anything."

—DENIS BOYLES, 52, PROFESSOR, WRITER, FARMER, AND FATHER TO THREE

TRASH TALK

"Respect the woman you're having sex with. Your wife. Your girlfriend. Whoever it is, just enjoy it and don't tell anybody. With me and my friends, you had a woman, and you came back to the bar and talked about it over a beer. That's wrong. I wish now I hadn't done that. I really downgraded a lot of women, a lot of good women. You should treat every woman as good as you treat your mother. You should show them respect."

—RONNIE COLE, 60, RETIRED BAR OWNER, BOUNCER, AND FATHER TO SIX

WHEN TO CHEAT

"When you're attracted to another woman, just ask yourself very simply, 'Is she worth leaving my wife and family for?' Few men would ever answer yes."

—RALPH HAAS, 63, RETIRED RADIO DISC JOCKEY, AUTHOR, HUSBAND FOR 36 YEARS, AND FATHER TO TWO

Sex without Love

"I got married when I was 37. I wasn't a virgin, and that plagued me because my religious background states that premarital sex is not acceptable. But the drive was in me for intimacy, and the physical part of a relationship is a large part of intimacy. So I couldn't say no. I wasn't strong enough. But what I realized is that the only premarital sex that was fulfilling for me was that which was part of a successful, psychological connection. Without there being love, there wasn't true pleasure."

—Jeff Linder, 52, commercial airline pilot
and father to one

How to Argue

"When most couples are having a disagreement, they aren't listening, they're reloading. They shoot and reload, shoot and reload. To keep from hurting each other, try mirroring one another. When your partner finishes speaking, repeat what she just said. Use her exact words; don't summarize in yours. Try to empathize by saying 'You make sense' or 'I imagine that must make you feel ____.' Then speak your mind and encourage her to mirror you in the same way. What this does is force the two of you to listen very closely to each other, and in the process, you'll start to feel heard, valued, and understood."

—Ed Shea, 53, relationship counselor and father to two

When People Change

"Marriages aren't made in heaven. They're made over a period of years of sacrifice, thoughtfulness, and work. The chief thing is that people change. They develop different agendas. They want to do different things, and you have to accommodate these differences within the relationship—where you live, how much money you spend, all these things. They have to be worked out. You have to communicate."

—Fred Matheny, 53, writer, former English teacher,
husband for 30 years, and father to one

SEVEN PREDICTORS OF A SUCCESSFUL MARRIAGE

"According to sociologists and demographers, you're likely to stay married if most of the following are true:

"You married after age 20.

"You dated for a long while before marriage.

"You are well-educated.

"You enjoy a stable income from a good job.

"You live in a small town or on a farm.

"You did not cohabit or become pregnant before marriage.

"You and your spouse are religiously committed.

"None of these predictors, by itself, is essential to a stable marriage. But if none of these things is true, divorce is a good bet. If all are true, it's likely you won't part until death."

—DAVID MYERS, PH.D., 56, PROFESSOR OF PSYCHOLOGY,
AUTHOR OF *THE PURSUIT OF HAPPINESS*,
AND FATHER TO THREE

A LESSON IN FOREPLAY

"A woman's passion works like an electric iron; it takes a while to warm up. A man's is like a light bulb. Remember this, and you'll avoid a lot of frustration."

—CHARLES KOVAC, 70, RETIRED CORPORATE VICE-PRESIDENT,
HUSBAND FOR 47 YEARS, AND FATHER TO SEVEN

HOW SEX CHANGES WITH AGE

"Sex changes over the years. When you're young, it's a very serious pursuit that's done largely for personal gratification. But as you mature, it develops into a form of intimacy that is to be enjoyed, sometimes with a sense of humor. The quality is better because no one is seeking to control anyone else, and there's more giving."

—ALFRED WILLIAMS, 64, FORMER PRESIDENT COUNTY JUDGE
AND FATHER TO THREE

NEVER DO THIS

"If you're married, don't ever be alone in a hotel room with a woman who is not your mom, your sister, or your wife. No exceptions. Don't stop by just to pick up the new sales data or drop off the old sales data. Forget the data, all right? Just don't go there. Period. Hotel rooms cry out for sex. It's against some law of nature for a man and a woman to be in one room together and not have sex. In fact, don't limit this rule to hotel rooms. Never be alone with a woman anywhere. This is the single best monogamy tip there is."

—HUGH O'NEILL, 46, AUTHOR, EDITOR, AND FATHER TO TWO

TIME AWAY

"The key to having a happy marriage is to spend time apart. Some husbands and wives are together all the time. Maybe they get along okay, but I think that when you're away from a person, you love them more when you're back with them. Even now, when I'm away from my wife for several days or a week, I love her more when I come back."

—RICHARD LAWRENCE, 71, CERAMIC ENGINEER, HUSBAND FOR 47 YEARS, AND FATHER TO FOUR

WHEN TO REMARRY

"If you get a divorce, be really careful about your next marriage. No matter how lonely you get, stay single for a few years. It's too easy when you're rebounding to try to replace what you lost and make another mistake in the process."

—JIM GORDON, 61, VIETNAM VETERAN, NURSE, SUBSTANCE ABUSE COUNSELOR, AND FATHER TO THREE

WHY AFFAIRS ARE BAD

"You sleep with some woman on a trip out of town. I've done it; it's not hard. But when you do, even if it's just a one-night stand, you trade away part of your soul. What you did is going to hurt someone down the line, or it's going to come back on you. We're constantly being tested throughout our lives, and despite how much you want to shrug off the indiscretions, you can't. You lose something when you cheat. You lose a piece of your integrity."

—JOHN F., 52, ATTORNEY AND FATHER TO ONE

REALLY BAD FIGHTS

"Never try to win an argument. Married people often see themselves as opponents rather than partners. They may fight unfairly with violence, insult, or withdrawal, or they may fight fairly with logic, emotions, or excessively good manners. But they're trying to win, trying to be the 'good' partner and prove that the other person is unworthy of them. Over time, this can destroy a marriage. Learn to resist doing this and, most important, learn to apologize."

—FRANK PITTMAN III, M.D., 62, PSYCHIATRIST, AUTHOR OF *GROW UP!*, HUSBAND FOR 38 YEARS, AND FATHER TO THREE

FIRST RESPECT, THEN LOVE

"Love is an elusive butterfly. Love can be here and beautiful one minute and then gone forever. We cannot control it. Should we try, it becomes lifeless. It dies in the hand of the collector. It becomes a memory pressed between the pages of a book. Relationships built on love have no solid foundation. On the other hand, relationships built on respect need never collapse."

—GEORGE SHEEHAN, M.D. (1918–1993), AUTHOR, RUNNER, PHILOSOPHER, AND FATHER TO 12

From My Father's Journal

"What is lovely never dies, but passes into other loveliness."

⚜

"If you love the good that you see in another, you make it your own." —Saint Gregory the Great

⚜

"Love cannot live without Faith; Faith cannot live without love."

⚜

"You must look into people as well as at them."

⚜

"Great strength comes from the heart."

⚜

"Love is the reward of love."

⚜

"All of us have a disagreeable person to live with, whom we cannot get rid of—ourselves."

⚜

"'I can forgive, but I cannot forget,' is only another way of saying, 'I cannot forgive.'"

THREE TYPES OF LOVE

"The ancient Greeks believed that there were three categories of love: loins, heart, and spirit. When you're young, you just have the loins going. But there are two other beautiful parts of love, which you become aware of as you grow older. I've been married for 30 years, and the love that I have for my wife continues to evolve. It has become a higher love, more of the spiritual kind of love. And I like that. Always try to remember that there are these three types, and cultivate them all."
—VINCE SPERRAZZA, 52, TECHNICIAN AND FATHER TO FOUR

THE CORNERSTONE

"It starts with learning the importance of making a commitment. Commitment to a job, even if it's a temporary one. Commitment to a sport, and not easily giving up. Commitment to anything you undertake, to see it through to the finish. If you understand commitment at this basic level, then you're better prepared for the ultimate commitment that you make to a spouse."
—JOE SCIORTINO, 66, RETIRED EXECUTIVE, HUSBAND FOR 35 YEARS, AND FATHER TO TWO

GETTING ALONG WITH YOUR EX

"I don't believe in divorce, even though I am divorced. When you marry someone, you promise to love them forever. And when I married my second wife, I invited my first wife to the reception. And I danced with her. And I told her that I still loved her. But I said that it's a different kind of love now. 'I love you as a sister, and I never want to see you in need. If you need anything, let me know.' And we're still friends. In fact, both my wives are good friends with each other."
—DON RANNEY, M.D., 67, PROFESSOR EMERITUS OF ANATOMY AND KINESIOLOGY AND FATHER TO FOUR

HOW TO MAKE HER FEEL SEXY

"A lot has to do with how you treat her on a daily basis. You score points for hitting the mute button the moment she starts talking (even if it's during *the* game), giving her back rubs after work, complimenting her on the way she dresses, kissing her neck, holding her, and, of course, saying 'I love you.'"

—ROGER H., 61, ARCHITECT AND FATHER TO FOUR

A MEASURE OF SUCCESS

"The truer the love, the better the sex."

—STANLEY V., 63, PART-TIME CABBY AND FATHER TO THREE

MAKING ROMANCE LAST

"If you find you are not feeling in love anymore, be more loving."

—FRANK PITTMAN III, M.D., 62, PSYCHIATRIST, AUTHOR OF *GROW UP!*, HUSBAND FOR 38 YEARS, AND FATHER TO THREE

SHOTGUN MARRIAGES

"Don't force yourself to love anyone. I've heard lots of men say, 'I'm going to get married, but I don't love her.' Why the hell would you want to get married to someone you don't love? There's a true love out there for everyone. You just have to be patient."

—RONNIE COLE, 60, RETIRED BAR OWNER, BOUNCER, AND FATHER TO SIX

YOU JUST KNOW

"After college, I began looking for a wife with serious intent. I got this idea to create a rating scale to better judge the women I was dating. Sex appeal was worth 35 percent; how good a Christian she was, about 25 percent; and so on, all adding up to 100 percent. I was seeing five girls at the time, and after each date, I would come home and update the scale. They were all running in the mid- to high-80 percent range. I loved them all.

"Then I met Janice. On our first date, we went to a movie and walked along the Ohio River. Something powerful struck me. Our conversation just flowed. She had no pretense. She did not try to impress me. She was just a beautiful young woman content with herself and very pleasant to be with. We did not kiss, but I did something illogical that night. I took out my rating scale, wadded it up and shot it into the waste can. It, and those other girls, were never seen again.

"Janice and I have been married for 37 years now, and we are very much in love. Some women are simply off the scale."

—JERRY SANDS, 61, PROJECT MANAGER AND FATHER TO FOUR

SAYING "I'M SORRY"

"When you find your true love, don't let your ego spoil it. Don't ever be too proud to say you're sorry. My wife and I were high-school sweethearts, then I went off to college. One day we had a fight on the phone, and I broke up with her. But I felt so bad, I hitchhiked 300 miles back home and went directly to her house. Only she wasn't home; she was out on a date. I stayed there and made her mother very nervous. When she finally got home, she was shocked. I told her what a fool I was, and that was the last of that. She was the person I loved, the person I wanted to be with. I had to do what I had to do. We've been married now for 40 years."

—BILL DEWEY, 62, FORMER PARTNER IN A GREETING CARD
COMPANY, SALESMAN, AND FATHER TO TWO

Why It's Called "Making Love"

"Making love helps make love last."
—Jerry Sands, 61, project manager and father to four

Joe DeCola, 60

He's unique among the fathers in this book because he is gay. And it took some time for him to realize it—specifically, 52 years, two marriages, and four children. But his story is more than one of simple sexual orientation. It has to do with finally finding yourself after more than half a century of searching. And, once done, how you begin again with family and friends.

Joe DeCola is 60 now, a jovial producer at NBC News, whose eldest son's wedding was recently featured in the *New York Times* society section. He accepts himself and, in turn, is more easily accepted. He has taken perhaps the greatest risk that a man ever can—not with his life or his wealth, but with what others would preceive as his very manhood. And he's not only survived, he's thrived.

Finding yourself: "The culture, your parents, the movies and television shows you watch, the books you read, all do a lot of telling you who you're supposed to be. When, for some reason, you know inside that you're not that person, it's a very scary thing. And this isn't just about being gay or straight. In fact, none of us are who we're supposed to be. In my case, I began to realize that I was closing more and more doors between myself and the people I loved. It's like you have this secret identity, and you can't just say, 'Oh, I'm going to close this door.' Because once you do, you end up closing door after door, until you're not there at all.

"I was compelled to admit that I was gay by the doors that were closing between me and my children. There was one kid in particular who was struggling so much with his own troubles that I could no longer avoid mine. And so, with a bit of luck and a lot of thought, I took some steps to change my life."

TRUTH: "My coming out was hard for different kids at different times, based upon where they were in their own development. At first, my youngest was saying, 'Oh, okay, whatever, Dad.' It wasn't until she began to come into her own sexual identity that she got angry.

"My eldest son, who was fully clear about who he was, told me that he felt betrayed. He was shocked and angry. I listened to him, acknowledged him, and told him I was sorry. That was the best I could do. His younger brother didn't speak to me for six months. He had to go off to Alaska and be a fisherman for a while.

"So it varies. And it also changes with time. As my kids got older and became more comfortable with their identities, my acknowledgment of my identity became less unsettling for them. I'm close to every one of them now. I love them. I think I became a better parent after I came out simply because I was more present. My kids even said so. In fact, I think that's the best thing you can do as a father for your kids—be who you really are all the time you're with them."

THE EASIEST THING IN THE WORLD: "Finding God. You just have to acknowledge that you need him."

THE HARDEST THING IN THE WORLD: "Change. Human beings are creatures of habit, and we feel safe when we're doing what is expected of us. For most people, being in a bad situation is better than being in an unknown one."

SEX: "It's about being present, being vulnerable, and being who you are."

DIVORCE: "It's painful. But try not to stay embittered. Do whatever you can with your ex to take care of the children. My second wife and I worked very hard at that because we knew how corrosive the situation is for kids. Nothing is harder on children in a divorce than ongoing anger and resentment, because they get stuck in this disloyalty crap. Even if you have an angry ex, don't add to it. Don't say anything bad about her in front of your children. Honor her and their relationship with her. After all, that woman is still their mother, and they need to love her and have her in their lives. That's hard to do if you're feeling hurt, but you have to do it."

RAISING TEENAGERS: "Recognize the fact that teenagers are looking to define themselves—their strength, their power, their self-esteem. And that comes from taking risks, not from being good. So help them take healthy risks. Encourage them to try out for a show at school, play an instrument, try a new sport, risk exposure, risk failing. Kids have to do that. It's part of growing up and being healthy. You can't find yourself without taking risks. But you don't have to jump off a cliff. You can climb that cliff."

BEING A REAL MAN: "Risk being vulnerable. Manhood is not about bravado. It's not about violence. And it's not about power. It's about courage, and being vulnerable takes courage."

REGRETS: "That I didn't have to be so scared. I didn't have to take everybody else's definition of me. I didn't have to be so accepting of who I was supposed to be."

Chapter 5

Fatherhood

My father never really liked fishing. In fact, he didn't even like fish, except breaded flounder once in a while on Fridays during Lent. Nevertheless, he'd wake up at 4:00 A.M. on summer weekends when I was a boy to take me fishing. Sometimes, he'd take a whole week of vacation, and we'd drive 12 hours to Canada, where I'd heard the lunkers lived. He even bought an old johnboat so we could finally get out to where I was always trying to cast. For a man who had never learned to swim, that must have been a titanic undertaking.

We fished all over eastern Pennsylvania for many years, but, come to think of it, I don't remember my father ever catching much of anything. He'd sit in the back of the boat in his white T-shirt and ball cap, working the motor or the oars so that I'd always have the best cast. He liked to drink 16-ounce cans of Budweiser because, for some unknown reason, it doesn't make you pee as much as other brands, and that was important on a boat as small as ours. He also liked eating salami sandwiches on a soft roll along with a fresh whole cucumber from his garden. You wouldn't think it, but there is no better breakfast on a hot August morning.

Although we must have spent months together in that boat, I can't remember having one noteworthy conversation with him about anything. You'd think that if a father wasn't fishing for fish, then maybe he'd be baiting his son. But no, he'd just sit there, his line spiraling loosely into the water, the net always within easy grasp in case I hooked the big one.

When I got to be 16, I started thinking that he was stupid and uninspired. And although I loved fishing more than anything else in life, I was glad, in a way, that we were floating far out on a lake, where no one could see his ineptitude or my embarrassment at it.

My father never really enjoyed playing ball, either. In fact, as my pitching arm got stronger and my curveball broke sharper, he became visibly intimidated during our games of backyard catch. Sometimes he wouldn't even try to get in front of the pitch, opting instead to let it bore to a stop in the thick bushes behind him. Nevertheless, most nights after supper, he'd ask if I felt like throwing. He'd call imaginary balls and strikes until the twilight made it difficult for him to see, yet never once was he the first to say, "Let's quit." He even bought a catcher's mitt so that he could be a more realistic target. And he volunteered as an assistant coach for all my youth teams. For a man who had never participated in sports as a boy and knew little of the rules, that was a gutsy play.

My father came to all my games, even when I was in high school and he had to leave work early to make it to fields an hour or two away. He kept my batting average, ERA, and other stats on white-lined notebook paper and updated them with the precision of an auditor. Yet when I look back now, I realize that he never truly loved the game itself. For him, there was no romance in the feel of fresh-cut infield grass, no seductive quality to the smell of neat's-foot oil rubbed into a new glove. He didn't have a favorite pro team, nor one article of clothing with a star player's number on the back. He preferred the stock market report to the box scores, and leaving early ahead of traffic to waiting to see if the Phillies could manage a six-run ninth.

At one Little League fathers/sons game, he was too ashamed of his athletic ability to participate. Instead, he stood out beyond the center field fence with his catcher's mitt, waiting for any home runs. I guess it was his way of taking part without risking any humiliating errors. But it hurt me nonetheless. I didn't understand how he could be such a fan of mine and watch all these games, yet never himself want to hit, to field, to throw, to slide, *to play.*

It wasn't until many years later when I had children of my own and my father was no longer around to fish or play catch with me that I finally made sense of it all. Of course he didn't love fishing; he loved how excited and happy fishing made me. And of course he didn't love the game; he loved me *in* the game. And that was enough. When you're alone with your son in a Canadian dawn, and he's concentrating on dropping his best lure next to a promising stump, then it doesn't matter if you are, too. When you're out back with your boy on a summer evening and he's trying to throw nine consecutive strikes to fan an imaginary side, it doesn't matter if you're capable of doing that, too. In fact, it's almost better if you're not, because otherwise you'd miss these magic moments, too lost in your own obsession would you be.

My father was indifferent about fishing and baseball and many other things he did with me. But he was smart enough to recognize that the activity connected us, and that it was a way to promote confidence, enthusiasm, and drive without ever having to lecture me on these topics. By first giving me the opportunity to sample the things that I was curious about and then supporting me unconditionally while I pursued them, he helped me discover for myself the power of having passion. And lest you conclude that my father was passionless, then let me volunteer this: After much consideration, I think that his passion, the thing that brought him the greatest enjoyment in life, was simply watching me be passionate. And I believe that's true for every father.

My young son and daughter are always saying, "Watch me." Whether they're coloring, playing, or creating, they seem to have an innate urge to be observed. Most times, though, I don't feel like looking. For some reason, I'm always more willing to watch for trouble than I am to look for delight. That is, until I remember my father sitting in that boat or standing in the first-base coach's box. I realize then that I don't have to be as enthusiastic as they are; it's enough for me just to be there. And if I can't find enjoyment in the activity itself, then I can, most certainly, derive pleasure from their doing it themselves.

It's easy to do what I want when I'm with my kids and then feel good about it afterward. It's much more difficult, however, to do what they want and feel equally satisfied. I believe now that my father was perhaps the greatest fisherman and ballplayer of all time, not because he was very good at either one but because he had the patience and wisdom to raise someone who was.

HOW A KID SPELLS LOVE

"You know how a kid spells love? He spells it T-I-M-E. You're showing love when you're giving that kid time. And that's how he judges you in the end."
—LOU PATTON, 70, RETIRED MANAGER FOR A COMPUTER FIRM
AND FATHER TO THREE

WHAT TO BUY YOUR KIDS

"When my sons were growing up, I was interested in carpentry, so I gave them tools. The problem is that parents usually give their children kids' tools. Even skilled carpenters can't do diddly with kids' tools. I gave mine professional tools. And they took care of them, too. To this day, they're all pretty skilled with their hands, and none of them looks down on any person or occupation."
—DEAN DIMICK, M.D., 73, PHYSICIAN AND FATHER TO SIX

THE SINGLE BEST THING FOR YOUR CHILD

"The best thing you can do for a child is to show him that you love his mother."
—GEORGE BOOTH, 78, RETIRED MINISTER
AND FATHER TO FOUR

YOUR STRUGGLE, THEIR ADVENTURE

"When my daughter was three years old, I was between jobs. I was her day-care provider because her mom worked and her siblings were in school. I had just finished getting an advanced degree, but I couldn't find a job doing what I wanted to do. So I was working as a handyman and driving a taxicab, and I was miserable because I wasn't fitting the role of bread-winner. But if you listen to my daughter today, she'll wax poetic about riding around town in dad's big yellow cab. Or she'll describe the jobs that she went on with me, like building fences and painting. It was a great adventure for her. That was the focal point of her young life."

—RICHARD LOUV, FROM HIS BOOK *FATHERLOVE*

LITTLE CHORES

"You gotta start 'em when they're little fellas—five, six, seven years old. Just give 'em little jobs, take 'em along so they help you. Pretty soon, they're big enough to run the tractor, and you can put 'em out there. I've seen it where kids didn't do nothing 'til they got outta high school. Then they didn't want to do nothing; they had their lazy habits."

—TOM BROWN, 53, FARMER AND FATHER TO THREE

THE MYTH OF AUTHORITY

"When it comes to children—my own three kids or the hundreds I had in class as a teacher—I've learned that you can't really tell them what they should or shouldn't do. Walt Whitman put it best when he said that a child goes forth each day, and the first object he sees becomes a part of him, whether for a minute, an hour, or a lifetime. The only thing you can really do is expose children to these things. They'll do with them what they want."

—CARL CAMPBELL, 74, RETIRED HIGH SCHOOL ART TEACHER
AND FATHER TO THREE

SAYING "I LOVE YOU"

"Tell your children you love them. Don't assume they know it. Say it. I fought in World War II, raised six kids with very little money, and back in 1984, I almost died when my lungs collapsed. But the most scared I've ever been was the night when one of my sons didn't come home. Since he didn't call, I really thought he was dead. And I hadn't told him that I loved him. We didn't hear until the next morning that he had been drinking and was picked up by the police.

"Just the other morning my daughter called from Colorado and the last thing I said to her was, 'I love you.' I can say that easily now, but for some reason I couldn't before. It took a lot of growing up."

—JERRY DOBEL JR. (1921–1996), INSURANCE SALESMAN
AND FATHER TO SIX

WHEN KIDS BECOME YOUR EXCUSE

"It is pathetically common nowadays for parents to use their kids as an excuse for not pursuing their dreams. Shame on them. The surest way to raise a spineless child is to be a spineless parent."

—MARK JENKINS, 40, AUTHOR, ADVENTURER,
AND FATHER TO TWO

NEVER LECTURE

"Never give a kid a lecture. Instead, tell him that you're merely imparting information he can do with as he pleases."

—MORRIS BRUCHES, 72, RETIRED VENETIAN BLINDS
MANUFACTURER AND FATHER TO TWO

SIGNS TO LOOK FOR

"There are two qualities that you should look for in your children: a sense of humor and whether they hang in there with a problem. If you see these two things, you needn't worry. They'll turn out okay."
—DEAN DIMICK, M.D., 73, PHYSICIAN AND FATHER TO SIX

HOW MANY KIDS TO HAVE

"You can have one kid and still lead essentially the same lifestyle you did when you were childless. Kids are portable. My daughter used to fit under a restaurant table; she grew up thinking that the stars were made of old chewing gum. But two kids—now that's life-changing. Two kids are twice the fun and four times the work. When you have two, the sides are even, but you're on the losing side. At three kids, your life is so profoundly different, you can't remember what it was like to have just one. Any more than three and you may as well throw in the towel."
—DENIS BOYLES, 52, PROFESSOR, WRITER, FARMER, AND FATHER TO THREE

CAUGHT CHEATING

"I was playing miniature golf with my kids. They were little at the time, and one of them changed their score. I told them that nobody will remember who wins this game, but everybody will remember who cheated. The same is true of lying. You're branded with these things. As it turned out, I have the most honorable kids you can imagine, although they didn't get it all from that lesson."
—WILFRID SHEED, 68, AUTHOR OF *IN LOVE WITH DAYLIGHT* AND FATHER TO THREE

A CHANCE AND A GOAL

"To keep your sons from drinking and chasing women, first give 'em opportunity, then give 'em vision."
—TOM BROWN, 53, FARMER AND FATHER TO THREE

WHEN I WAS A KID . . .

"Don't commit the mistake of trying to make a comparison to when you were a kid. You know the old story: 'When I was young, we did it this way. . . . ' That really doesn't pay many dividends. Instead, try to empathize, to understand what their problems are, what the peer pressures are. Things are not what they were 30 or 40 years ago. It's a different world, far more sophisticated, and you need to parent with that in mind."
—HOWARD VANDER CLUTE, 69, BRICKLAYER, FORMER NATIONAL COMMANDER OF THE VFW, AND FATHER TO THREE

A PLAN FOR NEXT WEEKEND

"Climb a mountain with your kids, any mountain. Pause at the bottom so that they can contemplate the immensity of it. Then tell them, 'Tomorrow, we'll be at the top.' It makes an impression on them, and it's a lesson that goes far beyond just climbing mountains."
—JOE DRAKE (1922–1998), ATTORNEY AND FATHER TO FOUR

SHOW AND TELL

"Show them the nobility of the horse, dog, falcon, and eagle. Show them the beauty of being in good shape. But most of all, show them the pride that you take in what you do."
—MORLAN NELSON, 81, WAR HERO, RESEARCH SCIENTIST, BIRD TRAINER, AND FATHER TO FOUR

HOW A FATHER'S LOVE CHANGES

"At first, men tend to love their kids conditionally because that's the kind of world we live in, a place where things are always being measured. But with age, you come to love your kids more like their mother always has, unconditionally. You gradually accept them for who they are, you stop trying to influence them, and you just support them. The Greeks called this *agape* love—love with no strings attached. It's the reason why the Unabomber's mother can be there at his trial. She doesn't see his imperfections, only the person she helped procreate, the person that's a product of her love. It's a strange but pleasant evolution for fathers—realizing that the reality of your relationship with your children is not what you thought when you first had them."

—CHARLES KOVAC, 70, RETIRED CORPORATE VICE-PRESIDENT AND FATHER TO SEVEN

SHUT UP ABOUT HEALTH AND FITNESS

"When it comes to health and fitness, don't tell your children anything. Instead, be healthy and fit yourself. The example is more important. I watched all three of my boys go through a period when they smoked and didn't exercise. I never said anything about it, although they knew I disapproved. But every one of them came around in their early thirties. They saw the senselessness of smoking and dropped it. They all started exercising regularly. To see something lived is more valuable than to hear it preached."

—LAWRENCE GOLDING, PH.D., 72, PROFESSOR OF KINESIOLOGY AND FATHER TO THREE

FRIEND, THEN PARENT

"I never threw a ball with my dad. Never once. And we never went fishing together or those kinds of things that kids and dads are supposed to do. We didn't hate each other. We just didn't do that stuff. And so, when I had kids, I swore that I'd do all these things and be their friend. But I learned that there's a danger in that. You have to always balance friendship with respect. Sometimes you want to go one way or the other. You want to be too stern or strict, or you want to be too much of a buddy. It's a tough wire to walk, at least it was for me. The key is being conscious of walking it."

—VINCE SPERRAZZA, 52, TECHNICIAN AND FATHER TO FOUR

PARENT, THEN FRIEND

"A lot of parents want to become friends with their children. But I want to remain a parent. I can be a friend anytime, to anyone. But being a parent means being a guiding influence in their lives. To me, that's more rewarding."

—BILL DEWEY, 62, FORMER PARTNER IN A GREETING CARD
COMPANY, SALESMAN, AND FATHER TO TWO

PUNISHMENT

"When a child does something wrong, your first duty is to help him see what makes it wrong."

—HENRY IKEMOTO, 74, RETIRED PROBATION OFFICER
AND FATHER TO FOUR

WHAT MOTIVATES A CHILD

"The best way to motivate a child is with curiosity. Say something new, say something different, and they'll be enchanted."

—MILLER QUARLES, 83, PRESIDENT OF THE CURING OLD-AGE
DISEASE SOCIETY, GEOPHYSICIST, AND FATHER TO THREE

YOUR SON, YOUR APPRENTICE

"Consider your son to be your apprentice in life. That's the way it used to be. The son was always with the father, either in the shop or in the field. So he learned from a very early age what being a man and a father was all about. Now we place more emphasis on our standard of living—having a nice house and two cars—than we do on training our sons. And that's starting to hurt our society."

—THOMAS KEMP, 53, RETIRED CORPORATE MANAGER, VIETNAM VETERAN, AUTHOR, AND FATHER TO THREE

FAMILY VACATIONS

"Travel with your children as much as you can. And don't stop once they get older. Even though my kids are grown and married, we still take family vacations. Everyone, including their spouses, goes on a cruise or something, just to be together as a family, to simply relate and love each other. It's still a wonderful way to hold and mold the family, even with the new members. It's the most effective thing we do each year."

—JOE SCIORTINO, 66, RETIRED EXECUTIVE AND FATHER TO TWO

STRETCH EVERY DAY

"Your job is to constantly be trying to get your kids to stretch, whether they're taking their first step or applying for their first job. Always be there as a safety net, but don't let them know it. If they're going to realize their full potential, they have to stretch, explore the possibilities and find out what they can do best."

—FRANK EINTERZ, 70, RETIRED VICE-PRESIDENT OF A FOOD-PROCESSING PLANT AND FATHER TO 13 COLLEGE GRADUATES, INCLUDING TWO DOCTORS, FOUR LAWYERS, TWO PH.D.s, TWO MBAs, AND A TEACHER

THINGS YOU CAN'T AFFORD

"If your kids want Nikes but you can only afford to buy them Converses, tell them to go out and raise the difference. They'll appreciate and take care of those shoes a lot more if there's some of their sweat in them."
—FRANK VIVIANI, 60, CANCER SURVIVOR AND FATHER TO FOUR

HOW KIDS RAISE PARENTS

"Never forget that the end product of child-raising is not the child but the parent. If you let yourself learn from child-raising rather than just trying to control or perfect your children, they can lead you through all the stages of human development from the other side and help make you aware of how men and women develop, how masculinity and femininity are taught and learned, and how to become a complete human being."
—FRANK PITTMAN III, M.D., 62, PSYCHIATRIST, AUTHOR
OF *GROW UP!*, AND FATHER TO THREE

THE DAD METER

"The father who laughs with his kids more than he lectures them is way ahead of the game."
—HARRY STEIN, 50, WRITER AND FATHER TO TWO

YOUR SHOT AT GREATNESS

"Fatherhood is the greatest opportunity in the world. To have children and watch them grow keeps you young. In my house, I have framed collages of my family at various stages of life. I stop and look at these pictures three or four times a day, remembering what a wonderful time that was in my life. Children are the greatest gift that God can give you."
—BILL BELL, 75, RETIRED MARKETING EXECUTIVE
AND FATHER TO THREE

DON'T SWEAT SCREWING UP

"Most men think that they have to be perfect when they're with their kids. This is not only too much effort, it's also a bad idea. Better you should just continue being a screw-up. Fall off your bike. Drop an easy pop fly. Order a really dumb product from some lame infomercial you saw on TV. Make a fool of yourself on the ski slopes. The sooner kids understand that you're not perfect, the sooner they'll realize that they don't have to be perfect."

—JOE QUEENAN, 47, WRITER AND FATHER TO TWO

NOTICE THAT MONEY ISN'T ON THE LIST

"The key to being a good father is providing love, schooling, and religion. If any one of these is missing in a home, you're bound to have trouble."

—RUBEN DOMINGUEZ, 86, RETIRED MANUAL LABORER
AND FATHER TO FOUR

PHOTOCOPIES OF YOU

"If you're a thief, the chances are very good that your kid is going to be a thief. If you're a drug addict, there's a good chance that your kid is going to be a drug addict. I quit smoking at age 35. Probably if I hadn't, my kids would smoke today. Your example is what counts."

—WESLEY PATTERSON, 66, CONSTRUCTION SUPERINTENDENT,
VIETNAM VETERAN, AND FATHER TO FOUR

GETTING A KID TO LISTEN

"Before a child will listen to you, he has to respect you. And the way you achieve that is by showing him that you're honest and sincere."

—TOM HAGGARD, 63, RETIRED TEACHER AND COACH, ARTIST,
AND FATHER TO TWO

From My Father's Journal

"When wings are grown, birds and children fly away."
—CHINESE PROVERB

❦

"Do not attempt to save your children from the difficulties of life; teach them to surmount them."

❦

"The very best medicine that a family can keep in the house is cheerfulness."

❦

"The object of teaching a child is to enable him to get along without his teacher." —ELBERT HUBBARD

❦

"To bring up a child in the way he should go, travel that way yourself."

❦

"When in doubt, say no. It's a lot easier to change a no to a yes, than vice versa."

❦

"Nothing has a better effect on children than praise."
—SIDNEY

❦

"The first duty toward children is to make them happy."
—BAXTON

A Case for Spanking

"I spanked my children. With 13 kids, I couldn't afford to be saying the same thing twice. There was a simple matter of keeping order in the house. But spankings were never done in anger; they were always by choice. Usually, if you give a kid a choice between being grounded for two days or being spanked, he'll choose the spanking because he knows it'll be over in a few seconds. I think that physical consequences are a lot more meaningful to kids. I don't believe in torturing them with sitting in a corner or being isolated. I don't like mental punishment. You should never threaten a child's mind."

—FRANK EINTERZ, 70, RETIRED VICE-PRESIDENT OF A FOOD-PROCESSING PLANT AND FATHER TO 13 COLLEGE GRADUATES, INCLUDING TWO DOCTORS, FOUR LAWYERS, TWO PH.D.S, TWO MBAS, AND A TEACHER

Those So-Called Child Experts

"When we were new parents, my wife and I had four well-developed logical theories on how to raise children. Then we had four children. One by one, those theories all fell. Now, I don't even remember what they were. Theories are okay as a place to start, but they don't take into account the huge individual differences in children. During the teen years and after, we just loved them, stood by them, and maintained a constancy in our love for each other."

—JERRY SANDS, 61, PROJECT MANAGER AND FATHER TO FOUR

Ask Your Children This

"Have you ever asked your son or daughter, 'If we could spend more time together, what would you like us to do?' Probably not—not if you are like most dads. Yet this is a fundamental question that has the potential to open our eyes to what our children really want from us."

—JOHN EVANS, 44, PSYCHOTHERAPIST, AUTHOR OF *MARATHON DAD*, AND FATHER TO THREE

THE FALLACY OF TEACHING

"I'm not sure that you can *teach* kids anything. I think they have to *learn* something. And there's a big difference. You can give them the opportunity to learn. You can give them the tools that will help them learn. You can give them a map or a guidebook to whatever it is they want to learn. But you can't force them to learn until they're ready. I like the Eastern tradition of education where the teachers don't teach. They just answer questions. They believe that if you don't want the learning badly enough to have questions, then you're not ready for the learning. Think about yourself. When you really want to learn something, you learn it very quickly. So when you're trying to teach a kid something, realize that you're just providing an opportunity for that motivation.

—FRED MATHENY, 53, WRITER, FORMER ENGLISH TEACHER, AND FATHER TO ONE

A SON ON DRUGS

"It took a long time for my wife and me to know that our son was doing drugs. He concealed it very well. He went to college and got into all kinds of trouble. I don't think he was there a year. Then he went to another college and got into more trouble. As a parent, it hurt. But while he was going through these trying times, we did not come down on him hard. We did not throw him out of the house. We did not tell him he was no good. We always provided encouragement. We did say, at one point, that if you continue these ways, you're going to lose your family. I don't know if that was the turning point or not, but he overcame these obstacles. My greatest satisfaction in life is seeing how well he's doing today."

—BILL DEWEY, 62, FORMER PARTNER IN A GREETING CARD COMPANY, SALESMAN, AND FATHER TO TWO

CONSISTENCY

"With kids, you have to be consistent. If you give in one time, they'll try the same thing again. I learned this as a counselor. When a kid came into the treatment center, I gave him a list of rules. I made him read them, sign them, and admit that he understood the consequences of breaking them. And if he broke those rules, he paid the price—no matter what. There was no such thing as an extenuating circumstance."
—JIM GORDON, 61, VIETNAM VETERAN, NURSE, SUBSTANCE ABUSE COUNSELOR, AND FATHER TO THREE

ADMIT YOU DON'T KNOW

"If you want to teach a kid something, let him see you struggle. When my children were younger, there were times when they'd ask for help with their homework—some science question or a mathematics problem—and I'd have to admit that I didn't know the answer. But I'd tell them, 'Let's dig into it, see what makes it tick, and learn together.' I think kids respond to that. I know that when I taught chemistry, I never had to ask any of my students to come and do research with me in the summer. If they knew I was doing research, they'd start hanging around, and before long, they'd ask if they could help. Then, we'd learn together."
—B. G. STEPHENS, PH.D., 63, COLLEGE ADMINISTRATOR, CHEMIST, AND FATHER TO FOUR

TWO PARENTS, ONE VOICE

"To raise good children, you and your wife have to be as one. That's very important. The father says no, the mother says yes. The mother says no, the father says yes. That's no good. You have to always support each other."
—H. T. BREMER, 64, CONSTRUCTION ENGINEER AND FATHER TO FOUR

THE MYTH OF THE SINGLE PARENT

"I had a hard time after my first wife died. Everybody said, 'Oh, but you still have your children.' Yeah, but on the weekends, this one goes one direction and the rest go another, and I'm all alone. But even though kids are supposed to have two parents in the house to grow up right, I don't think that's always true. If you stay involved in their activities and their lives, you can raise good kids alone. All mine turned out okay. You're worried, of course, because you're not always home and they're in the hands of someone else, but I think kids realize when you've got your back to the wall and when you're doing your best."

—WILL HESS, 70, RETIRED RAILROAD WORKER
AND FATHER TO FOUR

CONTROL

"No matter how mighty you think you are, you really don't have any power over another human being, even your own children. I had four boys, each a year apart, and it was a tremendous challenge. I wanted to raise them to be Renaissance men, good academically, athletically. But I overacted. I tried to control them too much, and things flew apart. Two ended up on drugs and one ran away from home. Once I backed off, things settled down. They're all college-educated now, and they all turned out to be Renaissance men."

—DEAN DIMICK, M.D., 73, PHYSICIAN AND FATHER TO SIX

WHAT CHILDREN NEED FROM A MARRIAGE

"It is not sufficient for parents to stay married for the children's sake; they must stay *happily* married for the children's sake."

—FRANK PITTMAN III, M.D., 62, PSYCHIATRIST, AUTHOR
OF *GROW UP!*, HUSBAND FOR 38 YEARS, AND FATHER TO THREE

BIG CHORES

"Don't be afraid to give your kids big responsibilities. They can handle more than you think, and it'll help build their confidence. For instance, when my daughter was 12 or 13, I put her in charge of the family checkbook. For three months, she paid all the bills, handled everything. And it paid off. She turned out to be a real sharp kid, highly reliable. Handles all the money in her family now."
—WESLEY PATTERSON, 66, CONSTRUCTION SUPERINTENDENT, VIETNAM VETERAN, AND FATHER TO FOUR

A + B = C

"Kids don't believe in the hypothetical like you and I do. They go by results. To a kid, what you see is what you get. So if you want your child to succeed, then you be the example. You have a decent home, a nice car, and a good job. You have the respect of your friends and neighbors. You have a good life. And you tell your child that this is what results from hard work. And they'll believe you because the proof is right in front of them."
—JIM GORDON, 61, VIETNAM VETERAN, NURSE, SUBSTANCE ABUSE COUNSELOR, AND FATHER TO THREE

CONSEQUENCES

"Help your children understand that when they do something stupid, there's a consequence. For instance, the first time my son drove by himself, he made an illegal left turn. I knew the police officer who stopped him. I could have had the ticket fixed, but I didn't. I made my son pay it because what he did could have gotten him killed, and I wanted him to think about that."
—RALPH HAAS, 63, RETIRED RADIO DISC JOCKEY, AUTHOR, AND FATHER TO TWO

BE A FAN

"Participate with your child in sports. Go to his games and help him develop his skills. Showing him that you think what he's doing is important will build his confidence."
—LOU PATTON, 70, RETIRED MANAGER FOR A COMPUTER FIRM AND FATHER TO THREE

HOW NOT TO RAISE A LAZY BUM

"Toss out or shoot out the television set. If you read, the child will read. If you exercise, the child will exercise. If you work, the child will work. If you watch TV, the child will become the lazy slacker you seem to be."
—FRANK PITTMAN III, M.D., 62, PSYCHIATRIST, AUTHOR OF *GROW UP!*, AND FATHER TO THREE

HIS DREAM, NOT YOURS

"Never impose your career ideas on your son. If he's not suitable to be an attorney, he might be suitable to be a medical doctor, an engineer, or a painter. Let him grab his own ideas, then try to connect with him along the way."
—RICARDO SUAREZ, 56, ATTORNEY, EL SALVADOR PRESIDENTIAL CANDIDATE, AND FATHER TO THREE

PAYING FOR COLLEGE

"Assure each of your children a college education, but don't necessarily provide all of it. Many times, children of parents who have oodles of money don't do as well in school as those who have to borrow or work. Not that any child should view finances as an obstacle to getting an education, but you need desire. Let them know that you're there to help, but don't just throw money at them."
—RICHARD LAWRENCE, 71, CERAMIC ENGINEER AND FATHER TO FOUR

WHAT YOU SACRIFICE

"Young couples often worry about how much sacrifice a family requires. But the weird thing is, there's no sacrifice in bringing up a family, even one as large as mine. It's like this: Which would you rather have, a Cadillac or a Lincoln? A family is an accomplishment. It never feels like a sacrifice."

—FRANK EINTERZ, 70, RETIRED VICE-PRESIDENT OF A FOOD-PROCESSING PLANT AND FATHER TO 13 COLLEGE GRADUATES, INCLUDING TWO DOCTORS, FOUR LAWYERS, TWO PH.D.S, TWO MBAS, AND A TEACHER

AT-HOME FINISHING SCHOOL

"Have you seen many kids lately surrendering their seats to old people on a city bus? Have you noticed *any*? Obviously, that reflects the general coarsening of the culture. All the more crucial, then, that you teach your son how to behave like a gentleman—how to treat people with respect, whether or not they deserve it. And as for your daughter, teach her to value those qualities in future boyfriends, bosses, and mates."

—HARRY STEIN, 50, WRITER AND FATHER TO TWO

WHEN THEY SAY "I HATE YOU"

"Don't pull back from loving your children during adolescence just because they pull back from you and your efforts to control, protect, or fix them. It is just when they hate you most that they most need your steady, reliable love."

—FRANK PITTMAN III, M.D., 62, PSYCHIATRIST, AUTHOR OF *GROW UP!*, AND FATHER TO THREE

TIGHT LIVING

"Teach your children to give up a little bit every day, to live tight a little bit every day. Then, at the end of every week, they'll have a little bit left."

—BENNIE MANCINO, 77, RETIRED INDUSTRIAL WORKER, UNION CHAIRMAN, AND FATHER TO THREE

PASSION IS INFECTIOUS

"Do things with your children that you like to do. If you like to read, then read to them. If you like to play softball, then go out and play, and they'll want to do it, too. Involve them in your life. Don't worry so heavily about trying to involve yourself in their lives, because if you're doing something and enjoying it, then they'll want to do it, too. I found this to be true over and over. It almost doesn't matter what I'm doing—working on the car, fooling around in the yard, or digging a hole. They'll want to do it, too."

—B. G. STEPHENS, PH.D., 63, COLLEGE ADMINISTRATOR, CHEMIST, AND FATHER TO FOUR

WHY SCHOOL IS IMPORTANT

"One summer when school was out, my son was working maintenance at the factory with me. Now that's a good job, but it's not what people count as a great job. Anyway, one day, he mentioned that he didn't think he needed to go to college, that he'd like to just stay at the plant and work. I said, go to college and get an education. Then, if you still want to work here, you can do it. You can always do a menial job with a master's degree, but you can't get a great job if you don't have the education. He's a commander in the Navy now."

—BILL BAKER, 68, RETIRED MAINTENANCE TECHNICIAN AND FATHER TO TWO

EARNING A CHILD'S RESPECT

"Respect is something you don't teach with a whip. You don't teach it with the back of your hand. You teach it with beauty. You teach it by creating something that's beautiful. And that's the relationship inside the family."

—THOMAS KEMP, 53, RETIRED CORPORATE MANAGER, VIETNAM VETERAN, AUTHOR, AND FATHER TO THREE

WHAT TO TELL YOUR KIDS ABOUT ALCOHOL

"Drinking is what gets people in the most trouble. But I'm not going to tell my children not to drink alcohol. Because if you tell kids not to do something, then they're more likely to do it. I am going to tell them that you have to control yourself when you drink, not to drive when you've been drinking, and especially to be careful about who you drink with. Picking the wrong drinking buddies can cause a lot of problems. Most kids don't realize that."

—RONNIE COLE, 60, RETIRED BAR OWNER, BOUNCER,
AND FATHER TO SIX

DON'T HIDE THE BAD

"Show your children the seedier side of life. I grew up in a very bad part of El Paso. Drugs were all over the place. I would take my teenage son to my old neighborhood and say, look, you see that guy over there? He's shooting up dope. You see that guy here? He's got AIDS. He's sharing needles with that other guy. And I'd tell him that I lost a lot of friends that way. I felt that I had to show him the bad part of life so he wouldn't end up there. It made an impression on him."

—LORENZO GAYTÁN, 50, VIETNAM VETERAN, SHEET-METAL
WORKER, POST OFFICE EMPLOYEE, AND FATHER TO TWO

SAYING GOODBYE TO YOUR BABY

"Whoever made the statement that a daughter will always be your little girl was right. Even though my daughter is 29, I still think of her as my little girl. But you have to be careful. You have to let her grow up. Realize that she's a young lady and that she's going to be all right."

—RALPH HAAS, 63, RETIRED RADIO DISC JOCKEY, AUTHOR,
AND FATHER TO TWO

HERE'S THE DEAL

"Give each of your children unreserved love and the reassurance that you will always be there as a father. Do your best to offer them opportunity. But, at the same time, emphasize that you expect them to be good citizens, responsible to themselves and the rest of society, and to ultimately make a contribution of goodness."

—JEFF LINDER, 52, COMMERCIAL AIRLINE PILOT
AND FATHER TO ONE

WHAT TO SAY TO THE GUY WHO'S MARRYING YOUR DAUGHTER

"Have a man-to-man with the groom. Issue an invitation. Make it clear that you'd like to talk to him before the wedding. This can take place anywhere. The point is to make him understand that you and he have one thing in common—you're both crazy about the girl. Let him know, without being explicit, that you expect, at the very least, sobriety, probity, fidelity, and an honest manly effort at husbandry. There should be two implications: First, you'll be watching and, second, he's got a friend if he needs help. Make it clear that you're both judge and ally."

—HUGH O'NEILL, 46, AUTHOR, EDITOR, AND FATHER TO TWO

WHAT TO SAY TO YOUR DAUGHTER

"Two weeks before the wedding, hand-write the bride-to-be a letter declaring your continued devotion. It doesn't matter if you've never written her a letter in your life. In fact, it may be better if you haven't. The letter should be short and simple, with the quality of a vow, a knight swearing fealty to the fair lady. It should make her feel watched over. Message: You are always in my heart; I remain at your service."

—HUGH O'NEILL, 46, AUTHOR, EDITOR, AND FATHER TO TWO

AWAY ON BUSINESS

"Being a pilot, I'm away from home a lot. Before I leave on a trip, I try to take care of all my responsibilities around the house so that my wife and daughter won't have to. Then, I make sure they know that I'll miss them a lot and that I can't wait to get back home, but that what I'm doing is important. And while I'm gone, I'll make frequent outreaches, usually by e-mail. When I return, I usually don't bring gifts for my daughter. That's because I don't want her to expect tokens. I don't want her to confuse the anticipation of Daddy coming home with his bringing her a toy. I want her to anticipate the joy of Dad's return as a coming together of family."

—JEFF LINDER, 52, COMMERCIAL AIRLINE PILOT
AND FATHER TO ONE

YOU'LL KNOW YOU'VE DONE ALL RIGHT WHEN . . .

"You get invited to your son's bachelor party."

—VINCE SPERRAZZA, 52, TECHNICIAN AND FATHER TO FOUR

Nick Rath, 54

If there is such a thing as a professional father, then Nick Rath perhaps comes closest. He is dad to 3 biological, 6 adopted, and 18 foster children. He has coached countless sports teams, been a scoutmaster, taught special-education classes, and counseled abused children for 15 years in Los Angeles County. Currently, he co-owns and operates a consulting business in Kingman, Arizona, called Joyful Parenting that "assists good parents in becoming great."

Rath, who often takes in kids with life-threatening conditions, has even had eight additional children (including three babies of his own) die. Nonetheless, when you ask him how he's doing, his reply will always be—to use his favorite word—"joyful." In fact, "If I was doing any better, I'd be twins."

LOSING A CHILD: "I believe that my children and I are one. We are part of a whole, which is God. Some religions, some philosophies, speak of it as being in the mind of God or being children of God, but however it's phrased, to me it's saying that we are co-eternal with God. That being so, what I really lost is the physical, everyday contact with my child. I have not lost that child. One son was alive for five hours in 1966, which is a long time ago, but I have not lost him. He exists. I can feel his presence every time I think of him. I remember him, his energy, his tenacity. I believe that he was a gift to me, a lesson for me, a blessing for me. And that gift, that lesson, that blessing never dies."

WORK: "My dad got up every day and went to work at a job in a jewelry store that didn't pay very well or emotionally reward him very often. But I never heard him complain. Instead, what I heard was, 'I get to work 12 hours tomorrow.' When I was young, I thought he was nuts, but as I started working myself, I came to understand that he was expressing his attitude about life. 'I get to' is so much more powerful than 'I have to.'"

FEAR: "When I was young, I feared almost everything. But I gradually learned to look at what it was that I was afraid of and what would happen to me if I did it anyway. Look at what your fear is costing you. Generally, it costs us our aliveness. Helen Keller said, 'Life is either a grand adventure or nothing.' I say, choose."

FINDING TRUE LOVE: "Hold a mirror up to your face, look at yourself, and say 'I love you' 10 times. Some people cannot say it even once, many are in tears by the fifth time, and almost everyone is affected by the tenth statement. Love is an assertion. If you start each day by looking in the mirror and realizing that love comes from you, not to you, you will never wonder where love is in your life."

BUYING A NEW COUCH: "Go to one of those huge furniture stores and tell each of your kids and your wife to go find the one they think looks best and will last 10 years. Then, when everyone has a favorite, go see each one and come to a family decision. Not only will this be a learning experience for the kids but it'll also become an ownership experience. That's not mom and dad's couch, it's our couch. And because it's our couch, we'll be less likely to eat slimy, nasty things on it."

BEING SATISFIED: "The universe is abundant. There are billions of stars. There is enough air to breathe, water to drink, land to live upon, and people to love, and there is an inexhaustible supply of joy. Speak about the abundance of the universe and not what's missing in your life. You can wake up to a world of not enough or a world of abundance. How you see and speak of the world is how the world will show up for you."

FATHERHOOD: "Instead of being a father, which is often a biological accident, become a dad. Children in the South often refer to their male parent as Daddy. To me, that always seemed to hold out more possibility for affection, nurturing, and sharing than just being someone's father."

LIFE'S MOST UNDERRATED: "The touch of another person. I've heard that it takes three hugs per day to maintain good mental health. I think that number is low."

LIFE'S MOST OVERRATED: "Doing. Although the term is *human being*, most people act as if it were *human doing*. It is extremely important that you develop your ability to *be*. To thoughtfully and quietly consider your life once, twice, or three times a day is of great value. The doing and accumulating of so many things is absurd."

THE KEY TO HAPPINESS: "The key to being happy is to simply decide to be happy, to decide that all the events in your life are either lessons or blessings. Most of my life, I looked outside myself for happiness. I expected my parents, teachers, friends, and then wives and children to make me happy. Looking back, I can see that most of the time I was not happy. Only when I finally understood that happiness was up to me did I become happy."

WHATEVER YOU DO, DON'T MISS: "Joy. Joy is the feeling of accomplishment that comes from doing something you consider worthwhile. Joy is the satisfaction of knowing that you've done the right thing. Joy is waking up in anticipation of another wonderful day. Joy is learning, teaching, sharing, expressing. Joy is being fully present to the moment. Joy is fully participating in life."

Robert Fulghum, 62

Robert Fulghum, author of *All I Really Need to Know I Learned in Kindergarten*, is one of America's most popular father-philosophers. Art teacher for 20 years, part-time minister for 34 years, and father to four, he started his professional writing career at age 50, and his books have sold more than 14 million copies. Nevertheless, Fulghum continues to live on a houseboat in Seattle, donate much of his earnings to charity ($650,000 in 1993), and write about those great lessons of the universe that we consistently overlook in our everyday lives.

BEING A FATHER: "What I tell my kids is that I may give you lots of beautiful words, but watch my life. There's a difference between fine words and fine living, what people say and what people do. My kids have said terrible things to me—that I'm old, I'm stupid, or that they hate me. But when I look at them, I see that there are a lot of my values that they continue to live out. Something stuck. And that comes through the example I give every day."

PERCEIVING THE POSITIVE: "As a former teacher, I had a lot of opportunity to look at the lives of kids whose parents said that things were going badly between them at home. But in the classroom, I didn't see them lying, being dishonorable, acting badly, or resorting to violence. Instead, I saw a lot of good things that they'd gotten at home. One of the most difficult things about parenting is that it's easy to lose track of the good stuff because it's the bad stuff that drives you crazy."

RAISING TEENAGERS: "The first rule is roll with the punches. The second rule is roll with the punches. And the third rule is roll with the punches. You're going to get punchy, but keep doing it."

KEEPING THINGS IN PERSPECTIVE: "The happiest and most thankful I've been in the last year was following 10 days of the worst crud flu I ever had. I was so sick that I thought, it's fine if I die. I finally realized it was over when I could sit up and have some chicken broth and crackers. Ordinarily in life, sitting up and eating soup and crackers is not a great thing, but this shows how contextual our sense of well-being is.

"There's an old story about a guy with terrible problems— 10 kids, no money—who goes to a rabbi and asks what to do. The rabbi says, get a goat and move it into your house. So the man gets a goat and moves it into his house, but life is hell. So he goes back to the rabbi and says, 'What now?' The rabbi says, get rid of the goat, and you'll feel much better.

"If you have troubles, look around and compare them with other people's lives. Be more thankful for it not being worse."

FRIENDS: "I've been playing poker with the same six guys once a month for the past 25 years. A thoughtful anthropologist would probably say that we're not playing poker at all. It's a men's group. We may not talk about things in the straightforward language of a therapy session, but we tell dirty jokes and lie. We may not beat drums, but we pound on the table and scream when we're dealt bad cards. There's a sense of brotherhood, of male bonding, that's really important."

MIDLIFE CRISIS: "I imagine that the first caveman went through a midlife crisis because he couldn't catch things he used to catch, his sleep got erratic, or his relationship with his wife changed. But life is always changing. *Midlife crisis* is a term that we've stuck on it, when it's really just a consciousness of the process of time and our finitude. What I always say is, if you don't wear your seat belt, that first accident is going to throw you through the window. It's going to be painful if you don't deal with life's issues early on."

HUMOR: "I am, when I look in the mirror, the most laughable and entertaining source of comedy in my life. Whenever I'm in a bookstore, I like to swap the philosophy and humor signs. We all need to develop the ability to laugh. Have a seriousness of purpose but a lightness of heart and never lose track of the comic strip you're involved in."

POSSESSIONS: "Owning lots of stuff is more a source of sorrow than joy. That's why I live on a houseboat. It forces me to live a simple life without a lot of stuff."

STAYING FIT: "When I turned 50, I shifted from high-impact activity to long-impact activity. I accepted that I am aging and that I will die. So I went from downhill skiing to cross-country skiing, running to walking, heavy backpacking to day hikes, playing squash to swimming. I didn't want to be one of those guys fighting age until they develop chronic knee and back problems. Good health has become more of an inner attitude with me than a physical ability."

NUTRITION: "I gave up fatty things, but if I found out that I had terminal cancer with six months to live, I wouldn't die eating hospital food. I'd go out in a delicatessen."

SUCCESS: "I was successful on my terms by age 50. Here's my criteria for well-being: good health; good group of friends; good love relationship; managing the finances so that there was a little more coming in than was going out; and meaningful work.

"You'll notice that there's no mention of being famous or rich. I had what I wanted before this Captain Kindergarten stuff started. It's like playing poker. I was having a good time, drawing average cards, and was ready to go home happily at 11:30. But I drew four aces on the last hand, and now it's 3:30, and I'm still at the table and high cards are still coming. But when the cards stop, I'll be just as satisfied as if I had left early."

Chapter 6

Death, Difficulty, and Despair

My father's father died the day I was married. The reception dinner had just ended, and the dancing was about to begin. The clatter of silver on china was being replaced by the clatter of chair legs on hardwood as the guests pushed back from their tables. It was that contented pause in all marriage celebrations when everyone tosses their linen napkin toward the centerpiece, pats their stomach, looks around, and smiles. This is family. This is good. We are blessed. That's when a waiter whispered in my father's ear that he had a phone call, a strange message, indeed, given that just about everyone he knew was present.

Everyone, that is, except his father—my grandfather—who had gotten ill a few days prior while out of town on vacation. But we had been assured that it wasn't serious. In fact, there had been a chance that he still might come. The news on the line, however, was not so optimistic. My father listened, dressed in a gray tuxedo that, more appropriately now, should have been black.

The band was raging and the dance floor was full when he returned. He went to his table, picked up his beer, and smiled. It was nothing, he said with a shrug, just a question about the bill. All taken care of. Not to worry. Is everyone having a good time?

Or, at least, that's what I surmised.

My father never told me or anyone else that day that his father had died. He danced genuinely with all who asked. He shook the hands of countless relatives, patted their backs, and joked at how far his son had come. He posed for an album's worth of photographs, standing tall and smiling proud. He waved enthusiastically as my new wife and I pulled away in our limousine, sipping Dom Perignon, the effervescence in our eyes.

And the next morning, when he drove us to the airport to leave for our honeymoon, he still kept his secret. He didn't want the greatest moment in my life to be spoiled by the worst moment in his.

Imagine that. Your only son, your only father. One begins, the other finishes. No space in between. No time to sort out what one means and the other meant. That's life, that's death. That's joy, that's sorrow. That's courage, that's fear.

One of my father's favorite sayings was "Take it like a Marine," and that he did. From him I learned that you don't have to be in the military to take a bullet. Every one of us sees active duty every day, and eventually, we'll all be seriously wounded. I wished that he had spoken about the pain, just because I wonder sometimes how it felt. But he probably taught me more by not saying anything. Not to have spoken or screamed or grimaced or cried, showed me that the hurt can be handled, that misfortune is never to supersede happiness, and that the bad must never be allowed to overshadow the good.

Three years later, my young son fell on our driveway, skinning his knees and nose. There was a moment of silence as he sucked in air to power his scream, but just before he wailed and the tears sprang, he looked at me and I made a funny face. I stuck out my tongue, crossed my eyes and pushed out my ears. So shocked was he that his pain was momentarily forgotten. He started to smile instead of cry and then, catching himself, he ran to me for a reassuring embrace.

For the first time, I remember feeling like I had made a difference as a father. I had postponed the hurt. I had in my arms a little Marine.

WHEN DEATH BECOMES APPEALING

"When you're really sick, when you know you're going, you accept death. There is no fear. I was given three months to live by my doctors. And there were times during the chemotherapy when I was pretty worn down. The pain and suffering was so bad, I would have accepted death if it had come. In fact, it becomes the easy way out."
—FRANK VIVIANI, 60, CANCER SURVIVOR AND FATHER TO FOUR

WHAT TIME DOESN'T HEAL

"They say that time erases everything, but not the real bleak things. I had two children who died from fever and pneumonia. That was 50 years ago, but I can still feel that sorrow even now. It's always on your mind. It's always in your heart."
—RUBEN DOMINGUEZ, 86, RETIRED MANUAL LABORER
AND FATHER TO FOUR

A CRYING SHAME

"There is a need for tears at the beginning of sorrow; that's the instant release. But to cry and not to gain is complete defeat. Pain is a teacher that must be understood."
—ROD STEIGER, 73, OSCAR-WINNING ACTOR
AND FATHER TO ONE

FAILURE

"Those who have not experienced failure . . . I'm not sure they're that successful."
—BILL DEWEY, 62, FORMER PARTNER IN A GREETING CARD
COMPANY, SALESMAN, AND FATHER TO TWO

From My Father's Journal

"Good things cost less than bad ones." —Italian proverb

❧

"Only in winter can you tell which trees are truly green. Only when the winds of adversity blow can you tell whether an individual or a country has courage and steadfastness." —John F. Kennedy

❧

"There are two kinds of men who never amount to much: those who cannot do what they are told and those who can do nothing else." —Cyrus H. K. Curtis

❧

"Fall seven times, stand up eight." —Japanese proverb

❧

"People who complain that they have had a lot of hard knocks during their lifetime probably don't realize that some of those knocks might have been opportunity."

❧

"The only people to get even with are those who help you." —B. Rothman

❧

"The true way to mourn the dead is to take care of the living who belong to them." —Edmund Burke

The Selfish Root of Grief

"I was sorry to see my parents pass away, but they were both very sick and it wasn't a productive life for them. I didn't have any grief because I had tried to be a good son. I had no regrets when it came to my parents. I think that a lot of people you see wailing at funerals are upset because they weren't good sons, daughters, or spouses. They're really feeling sorry for themselves."

—Paul Woehlke, 56, hospital administrator
and father to two

Live the Dream

"Do the things that you've always dreamed of doing *now*. Don't postpone them. My dad loved to be in the outdoors, but he was always so busy as a school principal that he didn't give himself that pleasure very often. He was going to do all his fishing and hiking when he retired, but he never lived that long. He died of cancer at 63. It was pretty wrenching to not only see him suffer so badly but also to realize that he had been cheated out of his dream."

—Fred Matheny, 53, writer, former English teacher,
and father to one

Relief and Guilt

"When someone who has suffered a lot dies, it's okay to feel relief. My daughter had cerebral palsy. She lived for almost 15 years, but was never able to talk or feed herself. She was just like an infant. It grieved me that she was never able to ask for what she wanted in life, even if it was only a drink of water. When she died, I felt some relief. At first, that troubled me; it made me feel guilty. Until I realized that it was just happiness for her at finally escaping the suffering."

—Bill Baker, 68, retired maintenance technician
and father to two

How to Tell If You've Lived Before

"There are subtle clues. Sometimes it's a déjà vu experience, a sense of familiarity when visiting a place for the first time. Or it can be some talent that you're born with that's already developed, like a young Mozart, for instance. Or you might have an affinity for some particular culture that manifests itself through the art that you collect or the books that you enjoy reading. Or sometimes, you might dream of yourself in a different time and place, which may not be a Freudian distortion but an actual memory fragment. These are just some of the hints."
—Brian L. Weiss, M.D., 54, psychotherapist, author of *Many Lives, Many Masters*, and father to two

A Father's Suicide

"Sometimes you can draw a lot of strength from someone's death. Sometimes you can use it to turn your entire life around. My father committed suicide when I was 12 years old. I had one brother and two sisters, and it was very hard for my mother and us. To help restore the integrity of our family name, I got involved in athletics. I won many honors and awards, even scored six touchdowns in one game. It built my confidence back up, and in the process, we became a very proud family. We learned the importance of togetherness and love. In fact, those things that happened early in my life made me work harder in my marriage and in raising my children so that they would never have their name damaged in any way."
—Bill Dewey, 62, former partner in a greeting card company, salesman, and father to two

QUICK EXITS

"It's always a shock when someone dies without warning. But watching people and their families suffer for endless periods, as I've often done as a physician, has taught me that it is a blessing for the person—only difficult for those of us remaining who love and miss them."
—THOMAS HOSKINS, M.D., 51, OPERATOR OF PROJECT CURE IN KENYA AND FATHER TO TWO

THE LIVING DEAD

"The more you're surrounded by death, the less that dying scares you. But there's a tradeoff; it makes you a very cold person. In Vietnam, I worked in a mortuary unit. I embalmed bodies and shipped them home. It's a job that most people can't fathom, and it affected me deeply. When I came home, I never felt like I could get close to my wife or kids. After seeing all that death, I didn't want to risk loving and losing anyone."
—LORENZO GAYTÁN, 50, VIETNAM VETERAN, SHEET-METAL WORKER, POST OFFICE EMPLOYEE, AND FATHER TO TWO

GO OUT RUNNING

"Let it come. Let it come. Death is just another part of life. But no nursing home for me. I want to die with my racing shoes on. Maybe finish a marathon and get hit by a bus."
—SAM GADLESS, 91, THE WORLD'S OLDEST ACTIVE MARATHON RUNNER AND FATHER TO TWO

TEMPORARY SETBACK

"Whatever you do, just don't stay failed."
—BILL BAKER, 68, RETIRED MAINTENANCE TECHNICIAN AND FATHER TO TWO

Where God Fits In

"You've got to believe in God. If you don't, then grief is pretty hard to handle. You've got to believe in the Hereafter, that there's something better beyond this Earth, that the Lord is testing your will. If you try to figure it all out yourself and try to cope on your own, you're not going to be able to handle it."
—Lou Patton, 70, retired manager for a computer firm and father to three

The Gift of Grief

"We adopted a baby girl named Samantha who died when she was four months old. It was a crib death. We put her down, and the next time we checked, she was cold as the devil. It was devastating. The death of a child doesn't make any philosophical or religious sense. I learned that among parents who lose children, more than 50 percent eventually divorce. That's because they're so devastated that they can't support each other. I was guilty of that. I was thinking about my own loss so much that I didn't support my other children or my wife.

"I was 39 at the time, coming up on my midlife crisis, and it made me examine myself a bit more. As it turned out, it was a starting-over point. I left the research lab to become chairman of medicine for a hospital. Maybe in periods of great pain and crisis, you get rid of the crap in life, the stuff that's totally meaningless, and refocus on what's important."
—Dean Dimick, M.D., 73, physician and father to six

The Worst Kind of Pain

"Emotional pain is much, much harder to handle than physical pain because it goes right to the core of self. You can't distance yourself from emotional pain."
—Wilfrid Sheed, 68, author of *In Love with Daylight*, survivor of polio, addiction, and cancer, and father to three

From My Father's Journal

"When man at the end of the road casts up his accounts, he finds that, at best, he has used only half of his life, for good or bad purposes. The other half was lost inadvertently, like money dropped through a hole in the pocket." —ALFRED POLGAR

❦

"When you get to the end of your rope, tie a knot and hang on." —FRANKLIN DELANO ROOSEVELT

❦

"If you ever need a helping hand, there's one at the end of your arm." —SAM LEVINSON

❦

"The difficulties of life are intended to make us better, not bitter."

❦

"Forget your mistakes, but never what they teach you."

❦

"Falling isn't failing until you stop getting up." —ARNOLD H. GLASCOW

❦

"No man ever sank under the burden of the day. It is when tomorrow's burden is added to the burden of today that the weight is more than a man can bear."

WHEN IT'S YOUR TIME TO GO

"Dying is the most fascinating experience in life. You have to approach dying the way you live your life—with curiosity, hope, experimentation, and with the help of your friends. Instead of treating the last act of your life in terms of fear, weakness, and helplessness, think of it as a triumphant graduation. Friends and family members should treat the situation with openness rather than avoidance. Celebrate. Discuss. Plan for that final moment. How you die is the most important thing you ever do. It's the exit, the final scene of the glorious epic of your life. Even if you've lived your life like a complete slob, you can die with terrific style. How you die will speak volumes about how you lived."

—TIMOTHY LEARY (1920–1996), HARVARD
PSYCHOLOGIST, COUNTERCULTURE GURU, AUTHOR,
AND FATHER TO THREE

THE DEEPEST WOUND

"You never completely get over the loss of a child. I lost a brother who was a fighter pilot in World War II. And I lost so many men in my regiment. In fact, I was shot three times myself. But nothing was as terrible as losing my son. He was killed in a drunken car crash at college. All you can do is say, 'Lord help me,' and try to carry on. You feel it all your life. Your only hope is to see him in the Hereafter."

—MORLAN NELSON, 81, WAR HERO, RESEARCH SCIENTIST,
BIRD TRAINER, AND FATHER TO FOUR

WHY IT HELPS TO HURT

"When your life is going nowhere in particular, there is nothing better than being knocked on your ass. Mindless mediocrity needs a hard right to the solar plexus. When you are in a permanent holding pattern, getting hit from the blind side may well be the best thing that can happen."

—GEORGE SHEEHAN, M.D. (1918–1993), AUTHOR, RUNNER,
PHILOSOPHER, AND FATHER TO 12

YOU ARE NOT YOUR BODY

"When it comes to death, think of yourself as a car and a driver. The car is your body. But we get confused and think that it's us, when we're actually the driver. When the car wears out, we'll leave it and get a new car. We are not our bodies; we are beyond our minds. That's the immortal part. Call it the soul or the spirit, but that's what goes on after the death of our physical bodies."
—BRIAN L. WEISS, M.D., 54, PSYCHOTHERAPIST, AUTHOR OF *MANY LIVES, MANY MASTERS*, AND FATHER TO TWO

YOUR LIFE PRESERVERS

"When you're down, look to your friends to bring you back. Open up to them. Ask for help. I was close to jumping off a cliff a couple of times in my life because everything caved in on me. Once, I even wrote a suicide note. Your emotional side is very fragile. It's like crystal. I was fortunate that I had friends who were very positive. They grabbed me by the ears and they helped me come out of it. Now I wake up and think, 'What were you trying to do, you fool?'"
—H. T. BREMER, 64, CONSTRUCTION ENGINEER AND FATHER TO FOUR

PAIN NEVER LASTS

"Pain is fleeting. If pain were that memorable, there wouldn't be many kids in the world. Women experience some of the greatest pain there is during childbirth, yet most still want big families. It's the same thing in athletic competition or anything else in life. You know it's going to hurt, you accept the pain, and you do it—sometimes again and again."
—BILL BELL, 75, RETIRED MARKETING EXECUTIVE WHO HAS COMPETED IN MORE THAN 200 TRIATHLONS AND 152 MARATHONS SINCE AGE 53, AND FATHER TO THREE

Why They Bury People

"When I was 15, I stole my brother's car and went joyriding with my best friend and girlfriend. As I was crossing a major boulevard in town, four other boys, who were running from the police with their lights out, hit us broadside. The girl was killed, and my friend was brain-damaged. The guilt eventually led me to quit school when I was 17 and join the Marines. By the time I was 18, I was in Vietnam and still so laden with guilt that I was almost stupid. I was looking to die.

"One day, my commanding officer asked why I had joined the Marines at such a young age, so I told him. Then he gave me some advice, which I still remember to this day: 'Here in the Far East,' he said, 'when you eat good food, you belch. When you make a toast, you break the glass. And when something dies, you bury it. That girl is dead. Bury her.'

"Well, I wanted to hit him. He was trying to take my guilt from me, all my reasons for joining the Marines, for leaving home, for leaving my childhood to come fight this war. I was really upset. But I sat there and listened because I respected him.

"My guilt stayed with me for a long time. In fact, it still haunts me, especially around Christmas because that's when the accident happened. But as the years wore on, I realized how truthful his statement was, that life doesn't go backwards, that life always looks ahead."

—Thomas Kemp, 53, retired corporate manager,
Vietnam veteran, author, and father to three

The Power of Persistence

"There's only one kind of person who fails, and that's the person who doesn't try enough."

—B. G. Stephens, Ph.D., 63, college administrator,
chemist, and father to four

LOSING YOUR JOB

"It happened to me when I was 45, and it was pretty traumatic. I put in 20 years with the company, starting as a salesman and working my way up to divisional general manager. I was one position away from my career goal, but suddenly it was gone. The divisional vice-president and I were on philosophically different planets, and he won.

"It taught me humility—big-time humility. And it taught me dependence on God. I did a lot of soul-searching and praying. But eventually, the phone started ringing, and another company was flying me out for an interview. I became the CEO of that company, and all kinds of great new things happened. It worked out a thousand times better. Somehow, it usually does."

—JOE SCIORTINO, 66, RETIRED EXECUTIVE AND FATHER TO TWO

FACING TERROR

"Fear is a bully that's within you. And like all bullies, you just need to look it straight in the eye and it will depart."

—VINCE SPERRAZZA, 52, TECHNICIAN AND FATHER TO FOUR

SOMETHING WORSE THAN DEATH

"During World War II, I flew 35 missions over Europe as a ball-turret gunner on B-17s. I never got shot down, but there were only five times when we didn't have some flak cut through the airplane. Shells would burst like hand grenades around us. And even though it was 60-below sometimes at 28,000 feet, there'd be sweat running down your back—cold sweat from fear, nervousness, and excitement. All you know at times like this is that you can still function, you can still move, so you must be all right. Fear is worse than death. At least death is peaceful."

—CHARLES VANBUSKIRK (1917–1998), QUALITY-
CONTROL ENGINEER AND FATHER TO TWO

From My Father's Journal

"Self-conquest is the greatest of victories."

❦

"Habit is a cable. We weave a thread of it every day, and at last we cannot break it."

❦

"The difficult thing is to avoid evil, not death. Evil, you see, runs after us more swiftly than does death."

❦

"The only safe and sure way to destroy an enemy is to make him your friend."

❦

"A small trouble is like a pebble. Hold it close to your eye, and it fills the whole world and puts everything out of focus. Hold it at a proper viewpoint, and it can be examined and properly classified. Throw it at your feet, and it can be seen in its true setting, just one more tiny bump on the pathway to eternity."

❦

"Don't wear your wishbone where your backbone ought to be."

❦

"There's a lot to see if you keep your head up."

❦

"Sympathy is never wasted except when you give it to yourself." —John W. Roper

How to Break Bad News

"Always do it gradually. In the medical profession, we lead a family into it by first telling them that things are not going well but we're going to do everything possible. In the military, they might first say that your son is missing in action. Breaking bad news should be a step-down procedure. It's important to give people time to adjust."
—JOHN HEISER, M.D., 66, PHYSICIAN, CLINICAL PROFESSOR
OF ANESTHESIA, AND FATHER TO FIVE

Keep Diving

"Don't let fear control you. If you have a great fear, stay with it. I had a fear of diving when I first got in the Navy, but I kept working at it until I got rid of the fear. And it can be done. It just takes persistence and some resolve."
—WESLEY PATTERSON, 66, CONSTRUCTION SUPERINTENDENT,
VIETNAM VETERAN, AND FATHER TO FOUR

A Spare Tank of Strength

"Don't worry. The resources are there to handle it. You have a spare tank that comes into play almost infallibly. Every year, you read about some athlete who has a crippling accident and becomes a paraplegic or a quadriplegic. In every single case, they handle it magnificently with a wonderful spirit. It's convinced me that there's a natural principle involved that supplies the extra strength to handle things like this. It's never as bad as you think it's going to be."
—WILFRID SHEED, 68, AUTHOR OF *In Love with Daylight*,
SURVIVOR OF POLIO, ADDICTION, AND CANCER,
AND FATHER TO THREE

HOW TO DELIVER A EULOGY

"When it comes to saying a few words about the dearly departed, remember that a eulogy is not just, or even primarily, a lamentation. It is a celebration of a life. Though it should certainly be reverent, a proper eulogy is never somber. We've all taken a blow, endured an enormous loss. But we're also left with the inspiring example of a life. The eulogist's job is to ever-so-gently start to fill the survivors' sails."

—HUGH O'NEILL, 46, AUTHOR, EDITOR, AND FATHER TO TWO

WHAT TO DO IF YOU'RE DIAGNOSED WITH CANCER

"The day the doctor called and told me that I had lung cancer was the day before my wife and I were supposed to leave for a week's vacation in New England. But we didn't cancel the trip. We went anyway. I suppose most people in that situation wouldn't have done that, but I've always found that it helps to have a positive mental outlook. After all, what did I really have to lose?"

—JAY WASILKO, 66, LUNG CANCER SURVIVOR
AND FATHER TO TWO

WHERE TO GO FOR PERSPECTIVE

"If you ever start feeling sorry for yourself, feeling that your life is hopeless, visit a children's hospital. I'm very active in the Elks Club, and sometimes we visit kids with cerebral palsy and other developmental disorders. I watch them trying to take a bite of food or lift a glass of water or write their names, and I think, hell, even though I've had three heart attacks, I'm in perfect condition."

—RALPH HAAS, 63, RETIRED RADIO DISC JOCKEY, AUTHOR,
AND FATHER TO TWO

One Man's Private Fear

"My fear is that the relationship of human beings to technology is becoming more important than that of human beings to each other."

—George Booth, 74, retired minister who was among the first military personnel to visit Hiroshima after World War II, and father to four

Fearless Finality

"I have seen death come many times in my role as a physician. Rarely does fear accompany it. People fight the thought of death, but when it actually comes, it is no longer the enemy."

—George Sheehan, M.D. (1918–1993), author, runner, philosopher, and father to 12

Fear vs. Faith

"When we had little money, we were not afraid. When we later gave away all our savings (only $500) to a new Christian ministry, we were not afraid. When our children have had troubles, sometimes grave troubles, we have feared for a while, but it is not a productive emotion, and we all need to move on to the potential for our lives. When I got Parkinson's disease some five years ago, I wasn't afraid. Our pastor says that sometime in the future, we will lose everyone and everything that we love the most. Life isn't just about gaining but equally about losing. Fear can help occasionally when we are low, but having faith in the Lord to see us through our last day makes a great deal more sense."

—Jerry Sands, 61, project manager and father to four

From My Father's Journal

"Discouraged? Remember: When Abraham Lincoln was a young man, he ran for the legislature in Illinois and was badly swamped. He next entered business, failed, and spent 17 years paying up the debts of a worthless partner. He was in love with a beautiful young woman to whom he became engaged—and then she died. Later, he married a woman who was a constant burden to him. Entering politics again, he was badly defeated for Congress. He failed to get an appointment to the U.S. Senate. In 1856, he was defeated by Douglas. One failure after another—bad failures—great setbacks. In the face of all this, he eventually became one of the country's greatest men, if not the greatest."

❦

"I felt sorry for myself when I had no shoes, then I saw a man who had no feet."

❦

"The world usually pushes a man in the direction he makes up his mind to go. If he strives to go up, they will push him up; if he lets himself go down, there will be plenty of people on hand to let him slide."

❦

"The most difficult part of getting to the top of the ladder is getting through the crowd at the bottom."
—ARCH WARD

Be the Eye of the Storm

"I was captaining a plane in Germany. My co-pilot was new, and we had lost an engine on takeoff. It was a stormy night, and I wanted to get back on the ground as quickly as possible. But the crosswinds were so heavy at 3,000 feet that I got blown off course. It was the first time I ever had to abandon an approach because of poor performance on my part. I felt a little pinch of panic, wondering if I had what it takes to land this thing.

"In situations like this, if you use the training you have and just remain calm, you'll survive. Our abilities are most reduced when we let stress and anxiety overcome our sense of confidence. And I'm not talking about being boisterous with confidence but rather just peaceful, knowing that you won't face a challenge that you're not capable of meeting. If you go through life with this presumption, then that sense of calm will allow your natural abilities to always come to the forefront and never be blocked by anxiety and fear."

—Jeff Linder, 52, commercial airline pilot
and father to one

Pain Makes Pleasure Sweeter

"When you live your life pursuing pleasure and avoiding pain, you only live half your life. The suppression of pain makes you insensitive, dull, rigid."

—Paul Rezendes, 55, former motorcycle gang leader,
author of The Wild Within, outdoor photographer,
and father to three

Phil Mulkey, 67

Shuffleboard and bridge? Forget about it. Phil Mulkey of Atlanta would rather pole-vault, high-jump, and set world age-group records in the decathlon. A former Olympic decathlete (Rome 1960) and father to five, Mulkey is the well-muscled, silver-haired Bruce Jenner of the Senior Olympic set.

What he is accomplishing is even more remarkable when you consider that in 1974, he was shot in the chest and lost his left lung. The incident stemmed from an argument over Mulkey's double-parked car. He admits that he "played Mr. Macho, being an Olympian and all," but his antagonist was unimpressed, grabbing a handful of shirt and firing an automatic into his chest. Mulkey says that he would have died if a witness hadn't called for help.

WINNING AND LOSING: "There has to be a little of both. If life is always winning, how can you ever appreciate it? Christianity tells us that in Heaven, everything is perfect. Well, I like to play pool. If I get to Heaven, break the balls, and all 15 go into the pockets, then I'm going to be gratified. But if this happens the next 48 times . . . see what I'm getting at? If you don't have the other end of the equation, if you don't have the lows, how are you going to appreciate the highs?"

ACCOMPLISHING THE IMPOSSIBLE: "You have to have goals—singular ones and long-range ones. I wanted to make the Olympic team badly, and it only took me 12 years of training to do it. If you're crazy enough, obstinate enough, dedicated enough, you can do almost anything. You just need the courage and patience to stay with it."

FAME: "I've achieved it, and it's been no small part of my motivation. Everyone likes recognition, but it shouldn't be the primary reason for doing something. We all enjoy using other people as mirrors, but sometimes we're so poorly aligned mentally that we can't see ourselves in them. If you want to be famous, then define how wide your circle is. You can be famous in your own home."

SEX: "Men are cursed in a sense by their sexual drive. Even when they lose it physically, they never lose it mentally."

WORK: "I had lots of jobs in my life—music, food, antique, automotive businesses—and I always applied myself hard. People ask me how I made the Olympic team. I tell them through 10,000 hours and 12 years of work. Then they ask how I ever applied myself, and I say that it was never really work to me. Work is a misnomer if you're really enjoying what you're doing."

SHORTCUT TO SUCCESS: "Reading. It's the only way we can come up with answers in the short time we have here."

FATHERHOOD: "Strive as valiantly to work and succeed with your family as you do with your career."

MEANING OF LIFE: "I'm here for two reasons: to learn and to have fun. If I can work the two together, then terrific."

AGE: "It's a curse in the U.S. that we don't venerate the old. There's a mistake here. We're missing out on benefiting from the wisdom that age and experience bring. There should be more retired people in the classroom, more elderly people in business."

REGRETS: "There were two very popular disc jockeys in Atlanta who were fired. An article in the newspaper said that it was the most devastating day of their lives. But three days later, they were hired by ABC in New York. Suddenly, it was the happiest day of their lives. You can't make a judgment on regrets until it's all over. Lots of things I didn't like happened to me, but it only leads to the next day, and you never know what that holds."

LIFE'S MOST UNDERRATED: "Time. We could accomplish so much more if we'd use our time more judiciously."

WHATEVER YOU DO, DON'T MISS: "Involvement. Life is all about this, getting involved in what you do, no matter how inconsequential. Suppose you start cleaning the kitchen. Pretty soon you get caught up in scrubbing the sink, the stove. . . . You're taking pride in what you're doing because you're so involved in it. I'm talking about a mundane thing here, but it's valuable because you're trying to do the best that you can. Involvement. Do that with other people, other things. There's joy in it."

Richard Hunter, 84

If age earns you anything, it's the right to rock the boat like you would an old porch swing. And over the years, Richard Hunter of Falls Church, Virginia, has become quite adept at it. The father to two was a conscientious objector during World War II, and when his wife of 33 years died during routine hip surgery, he questioned medical authority as well. Now, as the deputy secretary general of the World Federation for Mental Health, he's arguing by example that ability and age don't necessarily take divergent paths.

CONFORMITY: "Don't follow the crowd. Don't let somebody else determine for you what's fun or meaningful. There's no reason you can't go with the crowd, as long as you're able to *not* go with it at the same time. And if you choose to go, then have some say in where it's headed. Society is essentially a crowd, so you can't isolate yourself entirely. But you can find some place in it where something is happening, where you can be a force to lead."

TRUST: "In my opinion, inadequate medical preparation led to my wife's death. It taught me to be an advocate for my medical treatment, to ask questions. Doctors have a lot of the answers, but you need to get them to articulate them. There's a tendency to be awed by physicians and a lot of other professionals in life. You have to rely on these people, but don't do it solely because they have degrees from some medical or law school. Satisfy yourself that what's happening is right."

MARRIAGE: "I had a happy marriage for 30-some years. And they were very important years, when we were making a home, raising children, and building a family life. But then I reached a point where this wasn't as essential. Now, I find a great deal of satisfaction in my work. I would never have been able to do what I'm doing now if I were still married. You have obligations in a marriage that sometimes conflict with what you want to do. I'm not obligated to anyone. Although I may miss my wife very much, I'd be much more limited if we were still a pair."

LENDING A HAND: "You contribute much more by listening than by talking or giving advice. Parents need to listen to their kids more, then ask questions—not questions that imply criticism but questions that lead to defining the issues. This is not only true in dealing with children but also employees or anyone else you have a relationship with. Help people find their own answers."

MOST OVERRATED: "Sports heroes. Instead of worshipping the people who engage in sports, it would be far more beneficial to participate in sports ourselves."

READING THE FUNNY PAPERS: "Develop an appreciation for the ridiculous. The cartoonist can produce more insight in a single picture or strip than can come from an hour of unwelcome advice. By exaggerating the situations we find ourselves in every day, we can view our problems with humor and not be overwhelmed. I read the funnies every day."

Chapter 7

The Key to Happiness

My father and I went for a bicycle ride. Only we traveled much farther than fathers and sons normally do. In August 1990, we signed on for a three-week bicycle safari in Kenya, East Africa. I was 30 years old and was working as an editor for *Bicycling* magazine. He was a recent retiree who hadn't pedaled a bike in 50 years but desperately wanted to see the world and have an adventure. We had gone on fishing trips and other family vacations, but nothing like this. Those were childhood things, obligatory almost. This was the stuff of men, equals, voyagers, friends.

It was probably the riskiest, most illogical thing he had ever done. Africa is a disease-infested continent that requires a multitude of arm-numbing inoculations to even enter. Because of terrorist activity at the time, there was also a U.S. State Department advisory against nonessential travel to Kenya. Plus, it was just prior to the Gulf War, when the world's armies were massing to drive Saddam Hussein out of Kuwait. And here we were, two wide-eyed tourists from Pennsylvania flying directly toward it. When our Air Italia jet touched down in Jeddah, Saudi Arabia, in the middle of the night for refueling, I looked over to find my father praying the rosary.

I learned a lot about my dad during the next 20 days, more

so in fact than in all the years prior. Unfortunately, not all of it was good. I realized that the man I once regarded as all-knowing and invincible was not. He was terribly out of shape, couldn't tell the back of his helmet from the front, drank way too much beer, and was quite naive about the world. Often, I felt myself steering him through this exotic land the way he shepherded me through the Disneylands of my youth.

There was one day in particular that I recall a lot now. In fact, if it weren't for this memory, the stomach punch of his sudden death a short time later probably would have crippled me more. It was a ride that we did from Hell's Gate National Park, where you can pedal magically amongst giraffes and zebras, to Elsamere, the home of *Born Free* author Joy Adamson. It ended with a long, exhilarating descent. Although he nudged but 30 miles per hour, my father had never gone so fast on a bike. When we regrouped at the bottom, his knuckles were white and his face was flushed, but he wore a grin nearly as wide as the Rift Valley itself.

I think I remember this scene so often now that he's dead because I'd never seen him so alive. This man of 60 was a kid again, and we were neighborhood pals slapping high fives at our bravado and our conquest. How fitting that our destination that day was Elsamere, a symbol for life and freedom.

I wish I could say that my dad and I returned from Africa the closest of friends and that we spent many long evenings lost in pleasant reminiscence. But you know how it is. It's tough to find the time. The lunches and the Sunday rides usually got postponed because of the kids, the job, the work around the house. . . . It's funny how life can get away from you even while you're still living it.

But my experience with him on that trip taught me a lesson I've not forgotten to this day. In fact, that's why I made it a point five years later to take my wife and two small children on an 18-day bicycle tour of Ireland, and why we're planning to go on many more. It's the same reason I encourage everyone I know to invite their fathers, mothers, sons, daughters, spouses, or friends—no matter how far-fetched the idea may sound—to join them on a two-wheel adventure. After all, everyone remembers how to ride, but far fewer recall how to *feel*.

When you're traveling by bike, you notice things about the Earth and each other that somehow escaped you before. A bicycle tour crystallizes the world and the people in it. It feels just like emerging from a heated pool on a cool evening. It's a common, everyday, overlooked secret to happiness.

Adrenaline is also one of the few known antidotes to insincerity. Just as there are no atheists in a foxhole, it's tough to be phony on a bicycle. Perhaps it's because the mind becomes subservient to the body, which like any engine needs constant attention for high performance. Thus, there's little intellectual energy left for maintaining those walls we build around us.

I had thousands of dinners with my dad, but none quite like the one in the Kenyan village of Nakuru when we gorged ourselves on Indian food after a day of riding, and he surprised me with a birthday cake sizzling with sparklers. For the first time in a long time, I said thank you.

Likewise, I'd seen my father proudly struggle with many mechanical projects when I was a child, but he never seemed so lost as when his bike chain popped off on a bumpy dirt road near Lake Baringo. For the first time in a long time—perhaps ever—he said, "Can you help?"

Each fatherless spring since that trip, I've grown to love cycling more. Pounding through the furrowed farmlands of eastern Pennsylvania, glazed by the damp, stubborn coolness of a May dawn, I feel alive. I ride for all those who can't and, most frustrating, all those who have yet to try.

My father showed me that the benefits of bicycling run much deeper than physical fitness. What we've stumbled across is a basic world rhythm imitated by those pedals spinning round. There's a youth force living in the suspended energy of that age-old diamond frame.

Long ago, my father taught me how to ride a bicycle. I can still remember him running beside me, not wanting to let go but knowing that he had to. I'm proud to say that many years later, I returned the favor. I ran beside him in spirit on that long de-

scent to Elsamere, watched as his tentativeness was replaced by
a smile, and then I let him go.

BE SPONTANEOUS

"When I was growing up in Boston, we didn't have air-
conditioning. Some summer nights, it would be so hot that my
mother would say, 'I have to get out of here. Let's go to the
beach.' It could be 2:00 A.M., and we'd all get in my dad's 1950
Buick and drive out to the ocean. We'd sit there with the win-
dows down, just feeling the cool breeze, and I'd fall asleep.

"My family always did spontaneous things like this, and
they stuck with me. In fact, I try to do spontaneous things
with my kids, like showing up at school unannounced and
taking them out to lunch. No reason. 'You're just a great kid.'

"Just like children can be crazy and do something out of
the blue, adults can, too. Just because we're big people doesn't
mean that we can't be spontaneous. And I think that's one of
the secrets to happiness, having a bit of eccentricity and just
doing things."
—VINCE SPERRAZZA, 52, TECHNICIAN AND FATHER TO FOUR

GET SICK EVERY NOW AND THEN

"After each of my illnesses, I have felt not only undimin-
ished and unready to die but also quite goofily elated. Every
cheer comes with an asterisk, but so does every groan, as the
will to live keeps pounding back. And there's a certain excitement to be had just from living on the edge. You are more
fully alive than you have ever been, and getting more out of
each day. If the will to live can't have quantity, then it will
have quality, seizing on one great year in exchange for 10 or
20 dull ones."
—WILFRID SHEED, 68, AUTHOR OF IN LOVE WITH DAYLIGHT,
SURVIVOR OF POLIO, ADDICTION, AND CANCER,
AND FATHER TO THREE

STAY ATTENTIVE

"Stay in touch with the world. Never wear a Walkman. I hate those things. They distract people from the real world. Always be aware. Listen, smell, look around you. Try not to miss anything."

—GORDY SHIELDS, 80, RETIRED HIGH SCHOOL TEACHER
AND COLLEGE COUNSELOR, COMPETITIVE CYCLIST,
AND FATHER TO THREE

SAVOR A GRANDSON

"I had my grandson out at the house this weekend; he's going on nine. Had him up on the roof, helping us shingle. He was pulling staples, passing down roofing nails, getting us pop, and he was all dirty. It was a pleasure to watch him."

—WILL HESS, 70, RETIRED RAILROAD WORKER
AND FATHER TO FOUR

GET SWEATY

"Exercise is the most overlooked secret of happiness. Exercise produces neurotransmitters such as serotonin and norepinephrine that enable us to be happy. Exercise also makes us proud of our bodies, proud of how we look and feel, proud of what we can do."

—FRANK PITTMAN III, M.D., PSYCHIATRIST, AUTHOR
OF GROW UP!, AND FATHER TO THREE

WRITE A LETTER

"Every day in the mail, you get 16 catalogs, three offers for credit cards, and lots of bills. But you don't get very many nice letters. When it happens, you really appreciate it. You're impressed. Someone took the time, a half-hour maybe, to write me a personal note. You put it away. You reread it later. It makes you feel special."

—BOB MCCOY, 71, CURATOR OF THE MUSEUM
OF QUESTIONABLE MEDICAL DEVICES AND FATHER TO THREE

BE SIMPLE-MINDED

"A little food. A little wine. A cigar. Friendship. Being able to walk and enjoy nature. Watch the sunset. I like the smell of dirt after it rains, the humus. Today, there is very little appreciation of the basics. Most people are so brainwashed by modern technology and television that they overlook the simple joy of basic things."
—H. T. BREMER, 64, CONSTRUCTION ENGINEER
AND FATHER TO FOUR

STAND BY YOUR WOMAN

"My greatest joy in life is my wife, because no matter what I went through, she was right there. When I got sick and couldn't work, she went out and worked. She took care of the family. She took very good care of me. The only thing she wouldn't do was kill me when the pain got really bad and I asked her to. She's been there for 35 years for me, and I don't tell her enough how wonderful she is."
—FRANK VIVIANI, 60, CANCER SURVIVOR AND FATHER TO FOUR

ACCENTUATE THE POSITIVE

"When you get up in the morning and look in the mirror, don't say, 'My God! Is that me?' Instead, smile and say: 'I look beautiful!' That's the best medicine. Always smile. Always laugh. Don't be negative."
—SAM GADLESS, 91, WORLD'S OLDEST ACTIVE MARATHON
RUNNER AND FATHER TO TWO

WORK YOUR BODY

"Hard physical labor is the most underrated joy in life. It keeps you young in mind and body."
—SAM JERZAK (1924–1995), 26-YEAR ARMY VETERAN
AND FATHER TO SIX

BE A TRUTH TELLER

"What I've learned, based on 25 years of private practice in psychotherapy, is that lying is the primary source of depression, most anxiety disorders, most psychosomatic illness, most physical illness, and most divorces. If you tell the truth, the experience of being on the planet is a whole lot easier, less burdensome, more nurturing. It's a more loving kind of life. And it brings you more luck, more sex, more money."

—BRAD BLANTON, PH.D., 58, CLINICAL PSYCHOLOGIST,
DIRECTOR OF THE CENTER FOR RADICAL HONESTY,
AND FATHER TO TWO

SQUARE OFF THE CURVE

"I've been a runner for 30 years, ever since my mid-forties. Back then, I'd lace up my Jack Purcell tennis sneakers and run through the neighborhood. The neighbors laughed at me. They should have bought Nike stock. People ask me all the time why I still run. I do it because it allows me to eat all the pie I want, because it gets me out of hotel rooms when I'm on business trips, because I like to set annual goals and reach them. But the rock-bottom reason is because if you keep exercising, you can 'square off the curve.' That's what Kenneth Cooper, M.D., calls it in his book *Faith-Based Fitness*. That is, you can maintain high physical activity right up to the end of life rather than suffering a slow decline. He says that you may not live any longer, but you'll live better. That always seemed like a pretty good promise to me."

—RICHARD MOORE JR. (1923-1996), FINANCIAL MANAGER
WHO DIED ON HIS MORNING RUN AT AGE 73
AND FATHER TO FOUR

FOLLOW THE DREAM

"If you're often unhappy, ask yourself what you'd like to do for a living, regardless of income. Then see if there's any way to integrate that activity into your life."

—WARREN FARRELL, PH.D., 55, AUTHOR OF *WHY MEN ARE
THE WAY THEY ARE* AND STEPFATHER TO TWO

From My Father's Journal

"It is not wealth but tranquillity and occupation which gives happiness." —THOMAS JEFFERSON

❦

"Six ways to make people like you: 1) Become genuinely interested in other people. 2) Smile. 3) Remember that a man's name is to him the sweetest and most important sound in any language. 4) Be a good listener; encourage others to talk of themselves. 5) Talk in terms of the other man's interests. 6) Make the other person feel important and do it sincerely."

❦

"Success is getting what you want; happiness is wanting what you get."

❦

"A program for happiness: to live content with small means; to seek elegance rather than luxury, and refinement rather than fashion; to be worthy, not respectable; and wealthy, not rich. To study hard, think quietly, talk gently, act frankly. To listen to the stars and birds, to babes and sages, with open heart. To bear all cheerfully, do all bravely, await occasion, hurry never, in a word to let the spiritual, unbidden and unconscious, grow up through the common." —WILLIAM ELLERY CHANNING

❦

"A good laugh to a man is like oil to a machine."

❦

"Happiness has no price tag, but it's a neat trick to be both happy and broke."

GO NATURAL

"You probably won't believe it, but my greatest joy is to sit in front of the television and watch travel and nature programs. I love it because it's just like an open book. I can relax, drink a Coca-Cola, and learn so much about the world without even moving."

—RICARDO SUAREZ, 56, ATTORNEY, EL SALVADOR
PRESIDENTIAL CANDIDATE, AND FATHER TO THREE

MAKE A GOOD LAST IMPRESSION

"I remember Bob Miller, the man in the green suit, who was an Oldsmobile dealer at Bethlehem City Motors in Pennsylvania. He was a good businessman, an active churchman. I remember him saying at lunch on more than one occasion that his goal was to live each day as though he would meet his Maker that night. I always thought that was pretty good advice."

—ALFRED WILLIAMS, 64, FORMER PRESIDENT COUNTY JUDGE,
SURVIVOR OF TWO HEART OPERATIONS, AND FATHER TO THREE

ACCEPT YOURSELF

"You will never be young, pretty, handsome, popular, or rich enough, so don't waste your time trying."

—WILLIAM CASTELLI, M.D., 65, HEART RESEARCHER
AND FATHER TO THREE

LIFT UP YOUR VOICE

"I love playing the piano. When I was growing up, I was totally awed by anyone who had a talent for music. For me to have acquired that ability gives me such a sense of accomplishment and joy. My wife and I go to rest homes. I play; we sing. We try to bring a little sunshine to people who are confined."

—BILL BAKER, 68, RETIRED MAINTENANCE TECHNICIAN
AND FATHER TO TWO

BE SOULFUL

"We forget that we're made of body, mind, and *soul*. That's the important thing. We regularly take care of our bodies with rest and exercise. We regularly take care of our minds by reading and learning. But too many of us forget to nourish our souls. And the food that it needs is love."

—CHARLES KOVAC, 70, RETIRED CORPORATE VICE-PRESIDENT AND FATHER TO SEVEN

GET A HOBBY

"Develop something outside of yourself, a burning interest in Napoleon or the Civil War or anything that inspires the same kind of passion that kids have with ease but adults somehow forget about. I've never known an unhappy person with a stamp collection."

—WILFRID SHEED, 68, AUTHOR OF *IN LOVE WITH DAYLIGHT*, AND FATHER TO THREE

SEE SHADES OF GREEN

"I was driving with a friend through the Berkshires in early summer. 'When I took up painting,' she said, 'my teacher taught me to see all the different greens in a setting like this.' I looked at what had been until then simply a green expanse of trees and grass and foliage. And in an instant, I became aware of the infinite variety of greens that had previously been invisible to me. If you look, you see. If you don't look, you will miss more than the greens on the hills around you."

—GEORGE SHEEHAN, M.D. (1918-1993), AUTHOR, RUNNER, PHILOSOPHER, AND FATHER TO 12

DEFINE THE MISSION

"Many people have spent literally hundreds of hours working on mission statements for their corporations, yet few have taken any serious time to discover a truly meaningful reason for why they get up in the morning. Take some time to decide what you want your life to be about. What legacy do you want to leave? What is *your* mission statement?"

—DAVID McNALLY, 52, MOTIVATIONAL BUSINESS CONSULTANT, AUTHOR OF *THE EAGLE'S SECRET*, AND FATHER TO FIVE

EAT, TALK, LAUGH

"Whether it's a holiday or a regular evening meal, I'm never happier than when I'm sitting around the dinner table with my family—talking, listening, joking, and just loving. That's the most special time there is."

—JOHN HEISER, M.D., 66, PHYSICIAN, CLINICAL PROFESSOR OF ANESTHESIA, AND FATHER TO FIVE

CHERISH ENTHUSIASM

"There's an old saying that the journey is the destination. What it means is that how we move through the day is really the basis of our happiness. What we do is very important, but the bottom line, the foundation, is the spirit with which we do it."

—RUBIN NAIMAN, PH.D., 49, CLINICAL HEALTH PSYCHOLOGIST AND FATHER TO THREE

LEARN TO NURTURE

"I got custody of my son after my divorce, and I tried to be both a dad and a mom to him. He's grown now, but he took me out for breakfast this past Mother's Day. Even gave me a card. It made us laugh. It made me feel good."

—LORENZO GAYTÁN, 50, VIETNAM VETERAN, SHEET-METAL WORKER, POST OFFICE EMPLOYEE, AND FATHER TO TWO

STAY HOPEFUL ABOUT HOMO SAPIENS

"My greatest joy is meeting new people and learning about their worlds. I was very callous when I was younger. I didn't have much use for people. I was too self-centered. But life humbled me a couple of times—my business, my marriage. Now, I love to discover new people, new landscapes. It's a great pleasure. It helps make me a whole person."
—H. T. BREMER, 64, CONSTRUCTION ENGINEER
AND FATHER TO FOUR

TASTE SMALL VICTORIES

"Anytime your child or grandchild does something good, your head swells and you get a glow inside. And you can't beat that. I mean, I go to church for a baptism or when the grand-kids are in a play, and there's no bigger thrill than seeing them. I'm real proud of that."
—RONNIE COLE, 60, RETIRED BAR OWNER, BOUNCER,
AND FATHER TO SIX

TRY THE MIDDLE OF THE ROAD

"The key to happiness, the key to life, is being able to prac-tice moderation in all things."
—JOSEPH MCFADDEN (1922–1997), DIPLOMAT, PROFESSOR
OF JOURNALISM, AND FATHER TO FIVE

LOOK FORWARD

"The future is a good thing. Too many people today are too pessimistic. The best *is* ahead of you. Be positive about it."
—KONRAD SCHEID, 71, RETIRED FACTORY WORKER
AND FATHER TO TWO

From My Father's Journal

"The Supreme Happiness of life is the conviction of being loved for yourself, or more correctly, being loved in spite of yourself."

⚜

"Before we set our hearts too much upon anything, see how happy those are who already possess it."
—LA ROCHEFOUCAULD

⚜

"Some people are always grumbling because roses have thorns. I am thankful that thorns have roses."

⚜

"There is a wonderful law of nature that the three things we crave most—happiness, freedom, and peace of mind—are always attained by giving them to someone else."

⚜

"Briefly yet comprehensively, the world needs:
A little more kindness and a little less creed;
A little more giving and a little less greed;
A little more smile and a little less frown;
A little less kicking a man when he's down;
A little more 'we' and a little less 'I';
A little more laugh and a little less cry;
A little more flowers on the pathways of life;
And fewer on graves at the end of the strife."
—B. C. FORBES

ADMIT YOU'RE A FOOL

"The key to happiness is being able to step back, look at
yourself, and admit, 'I was an idiot. I did something wrong.'"
—RALPH HAAS, 63, RETIRED RADIO DISC JOCKEY, AUTHOR,
AND FATHER TO TWO

TAKE THOSE TWO WEEKS IN JULY

"Your happiest times are when you're on vacation with
your family. We went to Yellowstone Park on a camping trip
one time. Drove all the way out there from Indiana. Another
time, we went around the Great Lakes and up into Canada.
And we went to the Montreal Expo back in '67. Spent a week
backpacking on the Appalachian Trail, too. Another time,
we went to Disney World. There are just a world of
different things and activities and beautiful parts of this
country. It brought our family together, and the memories
still keep us close."
—RICHARD LAWRENCE, 71, CERAMIC ENGINEER
AND FATHER TO FOUR

MIND YOUR MANNERS

"Most people are in too much of a rush nowadays to be
polite. But it's important because it shows your concern, even
if it's only for a few seconds, for that other person. It's the simplest way to make yourself and the world feel good."
—PAUL WOEHLKE, 56, HOSPITAL ADMINISTRATOR
AND FATHER TO TWO

STAY HUMBLE

"To be humble yourself creates happiness in everybody."
—RICARDO SUAREZ, 56, ATTORNEY, EL SALVADOR
PRESIDENTIAL CANDIDATE, AND FATHER TO THREE

JOIN THE DAWN PATROL

"I've gotten up at 2:00 A.M. and driven to Washington, D.C., so that I could see the sun rise behind the Iwo Jima Memorial. And I've driven to the tops of mountains just to see what a sunrise looks like from up there. It's always glorious. The thing is, you can see one every single day, and it's always free. People don't put enough emphasis on the joy of everyday living."

—RALPH HAAS, 63, RETIRED RADIO DISC JOCKEY, AUTHOR, AND FATHER TO TWO

ACCEPT YOUR BEST

"Being satisfied with where you are is the secret to happiness. I don't mean being complacent. But if you're using your talents to their fullest and you're not reaching your objective, then just recognize that you're doing your best and be satisfied with that."

—LOU PATTON, 70, RETIRED MANAGER FOR A COMPUTER FIRM AND FATHER TO THREE

SPEND FIVE MINUTES ALONE EVERY DAY

"The most underrated thing in life is a quiet moment of reflection, time to take stock of where you've been and where you're going."

—FRED MATHENY, 53, WRITER, FORMER ENGLISH TEACHER, AND FATHER TO ONE

BE TRANSPARENT

"Let others see you the way you truly are. Take the risk of saying *intimacy* as "into-me-see.""

—CHARLES KOVAC, 70, RETIRED CORPORATE VICE-PRESIDENT, HUSBAND FOR 47 YEARS, AND FATHER TO SEVEN

GIVE PEACE OF MIND A CHANCE

"Everybody is too caught up in material things. Everybody wants lots of money, fancy cars, big houses, lots of clothes, long vacations. They have nine pieces of plastic that are all maxed out, but none of them has peace of mind. None of them can just kick back and say, 'Well, I feel good today. I haven't a worry in the world.' They don't have a clear conscience."
—JIM GORDON, 61, VIETNAM VETERAN, NURSE, SUBSTANCE ABUSE COUNSELOR, AND FATHER TO THREE

HAVE AN "IMPOSSIBLE" GOAL

"Mine is to find the longevity gene, cure aging, and live another 100 years. Having big goals, like going to the moon or traveling at the speed of sound, keeps you interested, challenged, and excited about life."
—MILLER QUARLES, 83, PRESIDENT OF THE CURING OLD-AGE DISEASE SOCIETY, GEOPHYSICIST, AND FATHER TO THREE

TRY GOD

"There are going to be times when your friends will fail you, when the people around you will fail you, when even your parents or spouse may fail you. So you have to have somebody you can talk to and turn to for strength."
—LOU PATTON, 70, RETIRED MANAGER FOR A COMPUTER FIRM AND FATHER TO THREE

LEARN, LISTEN

"The key to happiness is having a good education and a broad understanding. That way, you always have a chance."
—MORLAN NELSON, 81, WAR HERO, RESEARCH SCIENTIST, BIRD TRAINER, AND FATHER TO FOUR

CREATE SOMETHING

"Whether it's painting a picture, composing a song or building a house, I would never want my child or grandchild to miss the feeling of taking an inanimate object like a paintbrush, a guitar, or a piece of wood and making beauty from it. That's happiness."
—VINCE SPERRAZZA, 52, TECHNICIAN AND FATHER TO FOUR

ENJOY THE CAPRICE OF THIS CHANCE

"Whether you know it or not, you've already been very lucky in life. Your mother had an egg in her womb and your dad deposited about 20 million sperm in there, and one of those sperm got into that egg, and here you are. So just being alive on this Earth is a tremendous stroke of luck. Try not to forget that."
—MILLER QUARLES, 83, PRESIDENT OF THE CURING OLD-AGE DISEASE SOCIETY, GEOPHYSICIST, AND FATHER TO THREE

BE MOMENTOUS

"The essence of happiness is pausing to savor the gifts of our present moments. Happiness isn't in the future, but in this noon's meal with a friend, in this evening's bedtime story with a child, in tonight's curling up with a good book."
—DAVID MYERS, PH.D., 56, PROFESSOR OF PSYCHOLOGY, AUTHOR OF *THE PURSUIT OF HAPPINESS*, AND FATHER TO THREE

JUST LIVE

"I've seen people like moths, bumping up against the light of what they believe is the key to happiness. They're obsessed with getting it, but they never do. And I think maybe the reason is that it's not there for them to get in the first place. Once you realize this, I think you go about living your life the best you can, and happiness is a by-product of that."
—B. G. STEPHENS, PH.D., 63, COLLEGE ADMINISTRATOR, CHEMIST, AND FATHER TO FOUR

GET BUSY

"Happy people learn that happiness, like sweat, is a by-product of activity. You can only achieve happiness if you are too busy living your life to notice whether you are happy or not."

—FRANK PITTMAN III, M.D., 62, PSYCHIATRIST, AUTHOR OF *GROW UP!*, AND FATHER TO THREE

George Blair, 83

It must be a disguise. Otherwise, how could a man who claims to have been born in 1915 still be barefoot waterskiing, snowboarding, auto racing, and skydiving? Take off that white wig and mustache. Unzip that wet suit and show us who's really inside.

But doctors who have peeked within this remarkable body, including the father of aerobic exercise himself, Kenneth Cooper, M.D., tell us that it's no lie. George Blair is for real. And listening to his commonsense advice about life makes you believe that anyone could achieve the same. A proud father to four who routinely barefoots and snowboards with his grandsons, Banana George, as he prefers to be called, is the very personification of "a good old time."

THE ELIXIR OF YOUTH: "Adrenaline. Keep it pumping."

WORK: "Find something that engrosses you. Then, the harder you work, the happier you'll be."

RETIREMENT: "It's the absolute worst thing you can do. It's tantamount to death. It's a sham and a shame. What do you want to retire from anyway? Life?"

CREATIVITY: "The future depends on ideas, and imagination rules the world."

NUTRITION: "I never took a vitamin in my life, and I don't take any medicine now. I think you should be very careful about whatever goes into your mouth. Only put good, healthful stuff in there."

STRESS: "People wonder about me because I'm always doing so much and am so intense about everything. They think I'm under a tremendous amount of stress. Ha! The thing they don't realize is that if you enjoy what you're doing, like I do, then you don't feel any stress at all."

MONEY: "I've been a banker for 25 years. I make money by loaning money. But I think that people should live within their means. As soon as you start borrowing money, you're borrowing trouble."

THE KEY TO SUCCESS: "Focus. I don't care what you're focused on, but you ought to have something that you want to do in your life, in your day, and in this hour. It's awful to be out in the ocean just listless and being tossed from here to there by events or nature. You have to have a plan. Every day, I have an agenda that never gets completely done because I'm always trying to do too much."

EXERCISE: "Believe it or not, I don't have an exercise regime. I don't have time for that. Life is my workout. I get more benefit from *doing*, rather than getting ready to do."

Edgard Barreto, 61

Some men go back to college for graduate degrees. At age 61, Edgard Barreto went back to play football. He added 20 pounds to his 5-foot-10-inch, 165-pound frame and endured an entire season at Ohio's Ashland University. He never missed a practice, including twice-a-day summer workouts. And in the final two minutes of a game that Ashland was winning 28-0, he became the oldest man to ever play collegiate football. Oh, and by the way, he got two A's and a B in his three courses.

But such accomplishments are nothing new for Barreto, a native of Brazil and a former physics, chemistry, and biology teacher. He is in the *Guinness Book of World Records* for running 101 marathons in one year, which he did at age 56. When his daughters were 17, 19, and 21, he and his wife ran across the country with them—3,065 miles in four months. And in his spare time, he likes to do things like dig swimming pools with a shovel.

Give in to old age? Admit to the impossible? You've got to be kidding.

THE KEY TO SUCCESS: "Ant work. One grain at a time will get you there."

STAYING YOUNG: "You have to hang around young people—tell the jokes they tell, drink the beer they drink, eat the pizza they eat. To stay young, you have to regularly experience what it's like to be young. Otherwise, you end up playing golf in lime green pants and taking the poodle for a walk."

FATHERHOOD: "Be a teacher at all times. When you flip a switch and the light goes on, tell them what happened. I spent four months on the road with my girls explaining everything we saw, from why cows graze to why the sky is blue. Explain *everything*. Watch the Discovery Channel. The more they know, the fewer mistakes they'll make."

LIVING LONG: "Never retire. The minute you do, you'll start sleeping later, buying jugs of wine at the store, taking afternoon naps, and not pushing yourself. The discipline won't be there any more, your mind will deteriorate, and it'll kill you real quick."

MAKING A COMEBACK: "Never get behind. You don't have to come back if you're already there."

THE KEY TO HAPPINESS: "Keep reminding yourself that life is really very simple. You're born, you live, you die—just like everything else in nature. You're the one who makes it complicated. You're the one who makes it difficult. In essence, it's all so easy, so beautiful, so much fun."

Chapter 8

Regrets

My father could have been president of AT&T. I remember the opportunity. He came home from work one summer evening—garage door clattering up at precisely five o'clock—stripped off his tie and announced that he had something important to discuss. During dinner, he told my mother and me that he had been offered a high-level management position with Bell Labs in Phoenix. It meant more money, more stature, and, maybe even one day, a chance at the top.

It didn't impress me, though. In fact, I hardly gave the offer a moment's consideration. I was 11 years old, and my world was the corner of 10th and Hamilton Streets in Bethlehem, Pennsylvania, the steel town where I had been born and raised. "But what about Mark?" I asked, referring to my best friend next door. "And what about school? I'd have to change schools."

My mother was equally defensive. She had lived her entire life here, too, and had been settling in along with the foundation of our new house—deep and solid and sure. "I couldn't move," she said matter-of-factly. "I'd never want to do that."

And so ended the biggest day of my father's fledgling career.

Now that I'm the one pulling up the garage door at five o'clock and stripping off my tie, I can appreciate how he must have felt driving home with such news—satisfied and proud and brimming with dreams. Men of his generation were fiercely loyal to their companies, and they defined themselves by their jobs. "I work for AT&T" was never far behind my father's name in an introductory sentence. Thus, the chance for a promotion like this one was not only proof of his ability, but also an affirmation of his very existence. The job was his, as much as it was him.

After we delivered our callous verdicts, he was quiet. "Let's think about this," he finally said. He didn't try to convince us, nor did he get angry and order us to move. Rather, he just finished his meal as if it were any other night, changed clothes, and then went outside to pull weeds in his vegetable garden. My mother and I hadn't even congratulated him on being offered the promotion. We were too shocked and, I realized later, too selfish.

And that was pretty much it. My parents must have discussed it more, but it was always out of my earshot behind closed doors. Later, as I acquired more maturity, ambition, and work experience of my own, I found it hard to believe that he could have let it go so easily, that he could have listened to a sixth-grader and a housewife, whose only job had been as a seamstress in a brassiere factory when she was 17.

Although I did hear him throw it back at my mother once in anger, he never dwelled on what he could have been. He never used it as an excuse. He never blamed us. And he certainly didn't come to hate the job he was left with for the next two decades. But a large part of his ambition must have died that day. It was that moment all men anticipate, some with eagerness and some with dread, when you finally confront your dream and you must decide, once and for all, if you want it. To the young and the still dreaming, it seems an obvious choice. But to the middle-aged and responsible, it marks life's turning point.

My father chose his family instead of his dream. He worked out his days in the local plant, content with earning a good living instead of a spectacular one. He was dependable, productive, efficient, and well-liked. But after nearly 40 years of service, he was downsized by an early retirement offer that left him little choice.

After he left, I think he saw how easily he was replaced and how little difference he had actually made, and that wounded him.

While other men thrive in their retirements, he seemed to languish in his. He had all the trappings—the gleaming black Lincoln, the "Retired" license plate, the new golf bag, the eager grandchildren—but his heart wasn't in it. It's like the co-worker who changes jobs and moves away. Months later, you talk to him on the phone and ask how it is. "Great!" is his only possible reply because to say otherwise would be admitting a mistake, a failure. Most men are too proud for that. My father's job had disappeared and, in a way, so had he.

I always assumed that turning down the job in Phoenix was his biggest regret, that if he had one wish, it would have been to return to that dinner table and convince us to go. But there's another memory, just as vivid, that makes me think that it might not be so.

I was 12 or 13, and it was family night at the plant—the first time I had ever visited my dad's office. He showed me how telephones were built and how a voice is able to travel thousands of miles along a single hair-thin wire. He let me hold something called an integrated circuit on the tip of my finger, and he explained how this tiny chip would revolutionize the world (which it did). But the thing that made the biggest impression was not all this humming technology, but rather a simple framed photo of me on my father's desk. Here was proof that he thought of me at this place he went to each day. Here was proof that I meant something to him. Here was proof that he loved me.

Much later in life, long after my father had died and the opportunity to know the real answer had passed, it occurred to me that maybe I was wrong. Maybe his biggest regret wasn't that he hadn't become the president of AT&T, but rather that he had taken it all so seriously. I suspect now that the photo of me on his blotter was there as a reminder of life's priorities—an assurance that when his dream finally did materialize, he had made the right decision. The regret was that he didn't make that choice more often, that he spent 10 hours a day for nearly 40 years working for a machine that ultimately didn't care.

I used to be the executive editor of a flourishing magazine. I worked my way up through the ranks and proved my journalistic skill while still quite young. I could have moved to New York City and bigger publications, maybe even one day to the editorship of *Sports Illustrated* or *Esquire*. Who knows? But I resigned after three years because what I was becoming was not who I am nor what the important people in my life wanted me to be. Even though the bulletin board in my office bore photos of my wife and kids, they had become obscured by memos, Post-it Notes, and press releases. I couldn't see their faces, and they were losing sight of mine. So I quit, surrendered, said "No thank you" to a dream.

I once met a divorced, retired CEO who told me something surprising. He said that sometimes the most ambitious people in the world are those who say no. That's because it takes more talent, effort, and dedication to succeed with your family than it does with any business. Love is harder to amass than money. A career regret certainly hurts, but a relationship regret never heals.

On the desk where I write now, I have lots of photos of my family. But I don't keep them there for sentimental reasons. Rather, they're there to remind me of why I'm sitting in front of this computer in the first place. They're there to keep me focused, so that in the never-ending pursuit of those big dreams (which, yes, I still have), I don't lose sight of these little ones I've already realized.

And although my weekly paycheck still comes from a company, I work not for it but for myself. The great thing about writing magazine articles and books is that your byline is attached to each one. Everyone knows where it came from; everyone knows who created it. Unfortunately, my father's signature is on nothing but me. And I don't ever want him to regret that.

NOT TAKING TIME

"I'm sad to say that although I'm mechanically inclined, I have one son who doesn't even know what a Phillips screwdriver is. Because I never taught him. I never took the time."
—THOMAS KEMP, 53, RETIRED CORPORATE MANAGER, VIETNAM VETERAN, AUTHOR, AND FATHER TO THREE

THE SILENT TREATMENT

"The biggest regret in my life is all those times I gave my wife the silent treatment after arguments or disagreements. It doesn't accomplish anything. Eventually, you're going to have to say you're sorry. But in the meantime, you miss one, two, or even three days of talking with one another. That adds up. That's precious lost time."
—CHARLES KOVAC, 70, RETIRED CORPORATE VICE-PRESIDENT, HUSBAND FOR 47 YEARS, AND FATHER TO SEVEN

BEING QUIET, NOT COURAGEOUS

"What I've always really wanted to do, but never had the courage to do, is stand up in church and argue a few points."
—ERNIE S., 64, RESTAURANT OWNER AND FATHER TO THREE

ASSUMING SHE KNEW

"I should have told my wife that I loved her. I thought she understood that. But she didn't. And that was my mistake. I never said what I should have said. I was too busy. And we got divorced because of it."
—MORLAN NELSON, 81, WAR HERO, RESEARCH SCIENTIST, BIRD TRAINER, AND FATHER TO FOUR

LETTING HER GET AWAY

"When you're young, you think that nothing you do, no choices you make, will have a long-term impact on your life. But they do. After I got back from the war, I fell for a woman whose husband had been killed fighting in Italy. We really loved each other, but I couldn't commit. She had two kids, and I thought I wasn't ready to become a father. Like a fool, I started seeing another woman. It was my cowardly way of escaping, and it worked. I lost the woman I loved, and the other affair didn't last six months. That was 50 years ago, but the strange thing is, hardly a month has gone by in all that time when I haven't thought about her and regretted the path I took."

—JOSEPH GOLD, 77, RETIRED TEXTILE EXECUTIVE
AND FATHER TO THREE

THE END OF THE INNOCENCE

"I regret that my children can't have the kind of childhood that I had. On summer days, my pals and I would head for the woods, where we'd make these little bows and arrows out of saplings for hunting rabbits and birds. We'd fish and swim in the creek that ran along the south side of town. And sometimes our parents would let us sleep out in the field beneath the stars. They didn't have to worry, because it was safe. Everyone knew everyone in our little town. I couldn't imagine letting my kids do that these days. And I think they're really missing out on something precious. It's an innocence, a freedom from fear, that has totally vanished from our country."

—SAL MENKEN, 51, PERSONNEL DIRECTOR
AND FATHER TO THREE

THE PASSING OF PARENTHOOD

"I regret that my children grew up so fast. I don't know what happened to my life. It got gone too quickly."

—RICHARD LAWRENCE, 71, CERAMIC ENGINEER
AND FATHER TO FOUR

NEVER MAKING MUSIC

"I'm sorry that I never learned to play the piano. I can think of nothing better right now, as I'm nearing the end of my life, than to sit down and just manipulate those 88 keys. I would have gotten much satisfaction from that."
—JOSEPH MCFADDEN (1922–1997), DIPLOMAT, PROFESSOR OF JOURNALISM, AND FATHER TO FIVE

SHOOTING A RUBBER BAND

"It may sound strange to you, but I regret shooting a rubber band at a girl in high school. She screamed when it hit her, and I got expelled for two weeks. My dad couldn't read or write; he didn't even know what *expelled* meant. He just said, 'Fine, you don't want to go to school, you go to work.' And that was it. I never got another chance. I got a job and I went to work. I was good at figures. I was good at everything. I probably could have gone to college and been an attorney, but you didn't get a second chance with my old man. He just couldn't see it."
—BENNIE MANCINO, 77, RETIRED INDUSTRIAL WORKER, UNION CHAIRMAN, AND FATHER TO THREE

LOSING ALL MY HEROES

"It seems that every hero I've ever had has been exposed as a monster, a fraud, or a pervert. And every politician I've ever voted for seems to turn into a spineless, poll-obsessed weasel. I regret being foolish enough to believe in these guys. And I worry what we're destined to become once we're all too cynical to emulate anyone."
—CLARK GOODSON, 60, ORTHODONTIST AND FATHER TO THREE

From My Father's Journal

"Regret is an appalling waste of energy. You can't build
on it; it is only good for wallowing."
—KATHERINE MANSFIELD

❦

"I prefer freedom with danger to servitude with tranquillity." —THOMAS JEFFERSON

❦

"Too many folks go through life running from something
that isn't after them."

❦

"The only something you get for nothing is failure."
—ARNOLD GLASCOW

❦

"A man who doubts himself is like a man who would
enlist in the ranks of his enemies and bear arms against
himself. He makes his failure certain by himself being the
first person to be convinced of it."

❦

"So often we overlook the important while attending to
the urgent."

❦

"Be able to say to yourself, 'I have done what I could.'"

❦

"Act as if it were impossible to fail."

WAITING IN LINE

"*Nothing* is worth standing in a line. Time in line is time that's just plain wasted. 'Take my money,' said Thoreau, 'but not my afternoons.' I feel the same. Time is my most precious possession, and I do not use it fruitfully while waiting in line."

—GEORGE SHEEHAN, M.D. (1918–1993), AUTHOR, RUNNER, PHILOSOPHER, AND FATHER TO 12

NOT BECOMING AN UMPIRE

"If I had my life to live over, I'd try to become a major-league umpire. Although I played baseball for many years, I never had the ability to make it to the bigs, or even the minors, for that matter. But if I had thought of being an umpire, maybe I could have realized my dream. It really wouldn't have made a difference to me if I was behind the plate or next to it in Yankee Stadium."

—POPS HODGES, 73, RETIRED DELI OWNER WHO STILL PLAYS CHURCH SOFTBALL, AND FATHER TO THREE

AN OUT-OF-PLACE COMMA

"Too many people today are willing to accept mediocrity. Whether it's in our cars or in our leadership, we're too willing to accept it as the norm. My friends laugh and say, 'Hey, Ralph, how come you're so upset because there was an extra comma in one of the sentences of the book you published?' I try to explain it to them by putting it on their turf. Suppose you're a carpenter. Would you build a set of stairs that was a quarter-inch off? Well, words are my tools. I get very upset when there's a misspelling or an incorrect punctuation mark. Because to me, these mistakes are signs of my not doing the job right, of not having enough concern to do my best."

—RALPH HAAS, 63, RETIRED RADIO DISC JOCKEY, AUTHOR, AND FATHER TO TWO

NOT TAKING CARE

"I regret letting myself get so fat and out of shape that it took a heart attack to wake me up. Now that I'm exercising and eating smarter, life seems so much richer and more enjoyable. I can't believe what I was missing. I'd been dead for years without realizing it."

—JOEY COSCO, 51, GROCERY STORE MANAGER
AND FATHER TO TWO

MISSING THE WAR

"I was 18 years old, and the Japanese had just bombed Pearl Harbor. This was a war that was very describable. We knew who the enemy was. So I went down to sign up. I wanted to fly so badly. But the doctor told me that I had a bad heart and stamped a big '4-F' on my paper. I'd love to find that doctor now and show him what I'm doing."

—BILL BELL, 75, RETIRED MARKETING EXECUTIVE WHO HAS
COMPETED IN MORE THAN 200 TRIATHLONS AND 152
MARATHONS SINCE AGE 53, AND FATHER TO THREE

NEEDING TWO PAYCHECKS

"I feel bad that my wife has always had to work. I'm as liberated as the next guy, but I'd still like to feel that I can support my family the way my father did."

—JERRY RODRIGUEZ, 45, ROAD-CREW FOREMAN
AND FATHER TO SIX

ABORTING A BABY

"I want back the child my wife and I chose to abort years ago. At the time, I thought that I wasn't financially or emotionally ready to have children. But the fact is, you're never ready. You just have the baby and cope the best you can."

—JIM C., 50, GARMENT CUTTER AND FATHER TO TWO

Getting My Priorities Backward

"I had my job, going from 7:30 in the morning to 5:00 or 6:00 at night. Then, since I was involved in politics, I'd go to committee or council meetings. I overextended myself, and I had a nervous breakdown. It helped me realize that I had gotten my priorities twisted. My job had been coming first, followed by my family and then God. I learned that it should always be the other way around."

—Lou Patton, 70, retired manager for a computer firm and father to three

Wasting Time

"I regret wasting so much time. It's amazing how little value we put on it when we're young. I wasted so much time staring at junk on television, reading dumb books, talking about unimportant things with people I didn't particularly like, chasing women I never caught. When you get older, time gets a lot more valuable, and you start thinking about all the things that you wanted to do with your life that you could have done if you'd used your free time a little more productively. At least if I'd spent it golfing, I would have broken 100 by now."

—Mike Strehren, 68, photographer and father to three

Going Deaf

"When I came back from Vietnam, I was an introvert. To me, shutting the blinds, turning on the light, and listening to music or reading a book was my way of relaxing. My wife would say, we need to go here, we need to go there. And I'd say, go ahead, take off. One day, she said we need to go to counseling. But I was stubborn and I refused. I thought everything was all right. It wasn't. We got divorced after 16½ years. I learned that you need to listen to what your wife is saying. You need to listen when she says, 'Hey, there's a problem here.'"

—Lorenzo Gaytán, 50, Vietnam veteran, sheet-metal worker, post office employee, and father to two

MISSPENDING MONEY

"If I had all the money I ever made and threw away, I would be a millionaire twice over. I'm pretty well-off right now, but if I could've kept all that money, everything I gambled away, drank, and spent on women and cars, it would really amount to something."

—RONNIE COLE, 60, RETIRED BAR OWNER, BOUNCER, AND FATHER TO SIX

DUSTING THE TROPHIES

"I used to be so proud of the trophies I'd won until I realized that trophies are of little consequence. A race is won and forgotten. The trophy is received and rusts on a shelf. There is nothing briefer than the laurel. 'So soon they forget,' you will say. But so soon *you* will forget as well. The memorable thing is not to excel against others but to excel against yourself."

—GEORGE SHEEHAN, M.D. (1918–1993), AUTHOR, RUNNER, PHILOSOPHER, AND FATHER TO 12

NEVER BEING A MR.

"I'm sorry that I didn't continue in school. I dropped out in the sixth grade. You can only bump your way up so much without schooling before you hit a brick wall. If I would've had at least a high school diploma, I would've been 'Mr. Dominguez' instead of just 'Hey, Ruben.'"

—RUBEN DOMINGUEZ, 86, RETIRED MANUAL LABORER AND FATHER TO FOUR

THE DEMISE OF CHILDHOOD

"I'm sad that a lot of children these days miss being children. We make them become young adults too quickly. I believe that only one parent in the family should work, if it's at all possible. Someone has to be home with the child so it can be a child."

—FRANK VIVIANI, 60, CANCER SURVIVOR AND FATHER TO FOUR

Not Beating Up Tommy Rocca

"The bastard sat behind me in algebra. He used to flick my ears and shoot spitballs into my hair. I'd tell him to stop, but he'd just laugh and keep doing it. It went on for months. I used to dream of turning around and punching him in the head, but I never did. I was afraid I'd get in too much trouble since he was a varsity wrestler and I was only in the band."

—Oscar Garcieu, 51, bank vice-president and father to five

Telling My Son to Get Out

"I told my son to get out and he did. I haven't seen or heard from him in four years. Maybe fate will have him read this. And if it does, I want him to know that I was wrong, I'm sorry, and nothing would make me happier than to have him back."

—Elias Stoneback, 53, architect and father to three

Getting Divorced

"My biggest regret is that my first marriage didn't work out, and that I couldn't raise my kids from bottom to top in one family. I think it would have made a difference in their lives if I'd been able to do that. I think it would have given them a different perspective on marriage, divorce, and raising children. Two of my kids are divorced themselves."

—Jim Gordon, 61, Vietnam veteran, nurse, substance abuse counselor, and father to three

From My Father's Journal

"There is a calculated risk in everything. There has been a calculated risk in every stage of American development. The nation was built by men who took risks—pioneers who were not afraid of the wilderness, businessmen who were not afraid of failures, scientists who were not afraid of the truth, thinkers who were not afraid of action."

⸙

"A failure is a man who has blundered and then is not able to cash in on the experience."

⸙

"There are two tragedies in life. One is not to get your heart's desire. The other is to get it."
—GEORGE BERNARD SHAW

⸙

"Lack of something to feel important about is almost the greatest tragedy a man may have."
—DR. A. E. MORGAN

⸙

"The tragedy of life is not so much what men suffer, but rather what they miss." —THOMAS CARLYLE

⸙

"Do not attempt to do a thing unless you are sure of yourself; but do not relinquish it simply because someone else is not sure of you."

Never Finding Him

"I tried to find out who the man was who stood in front of that tank in Tiananmen Square. I wrote to the newspaper that ran the photo. I wrote to the Chinese Embassy in Washington, D.C. Nobody knew. When the government was bringing those tanks in to overthrow the riot, he stood right in front of them. He stopped them. Man, that took guts. All that tank driver had to do was throw it in gear and run him over, and he'd be a forgotten casualty. But he stopped them. His people were fighting for democracy, and this guy did his part. I would love to meet someone with that much conviction and courage."

—Lorenzo Gaytán, 50, Vietnam veteran, sheet-metal worker, post office employee, and father to two

Taking Mom and Dad for Granted

"It isn't until you are a parent and have raised a family that you recognize how important your parents were and, in my case, how little I expressed my love to them. That's the one thing that I wish I could do over again. I wish I could tell my parents how much they meant to me."

—Frank Einterz, 70, retired vice-president of a food-processing plant and father to 13

Hitting My Wife

"Before I knew it, my hand shot out and I hit her in the face. I was angry, I had been drinking, and she said something that really hurt me. But that was still no excuse for what I did. I told her that I was sorry. I kissed the bruise. But it has never fully healed, in her or in me."

—Blaine C., 47, automobile salesman and father to one

Norman Vaughan, 93

In 1929, Norman Vaughan was part of Admiral Richard Byrd's expedition to the South Pole. In fact, Byrd named an Antarctic peak—Mount Vaughan—in his honor. In 1994, a few days before his 89th birthday, Norman realized a dream by climbing to the summit of this 10,302-foot ice-covered mountain.

This was only the latest in a lifelong string of adventures for Vaughan, a gregarious father to two who dropped out of Harvard, sold chainsaws to lumberjacks, was decorated for numerous heroic search-and-rescue missions during World War II, competed in 13 Iditarod sled-dog races, taught Pope John Paul II to mush, has been married four times (most recently at 82), and published an autobiography aptly titled *My Life of Adventure*.

THRILLS: "Most men have zero adventure in their lives, and that's sad because it takes you away from the humdrum of life and helps you see other people's points of view. Some men go on these fancy two-week bicycling trips. They come back and say they had a great time, but it's still just a bike trip. An adventure is not knowing which way you'll go on that bicycle. You come to a corner and see some trees in the distance, so you take that road. Then you see a brook, so you go that way, and you end up fishing with a fellow you meet. That's adventure, facing the future without any given plan. Try it. It'll make you feel great!"

DIVORCE: "I've been through it three times. If you're not happy, and you realize you never will be even if things straighten out a bit, then it's best to correct it. If you do this early and don't wait until it's forced on you, then you'll end up being comfortably associated with your former spouse. If children or money is involved, settlement won't be vicious. A vicious attitude can lead to far greater adverse circumstances."

FATHERHOOD: "If a man is too busy with his hobbies or business to devote time to his children, then he is doing himself and them a disservice. A father should strike away from his

normal life habits on occasion to back up his son at football games, hockey games, or whatever activities he participates in. He will be a spectator, but the son will be confident that he loves him and supports him. The child doesn't have to be a champion. In fact, it's a father's backing of love at the moment of defeat that's most important."

MONEY: "Turn your profits into pleasures for yourself and your family. Spend it. The man who saves his money for emergencies is doing the right thing. But the one who hoards it like a miser, turning it over and over every week, is making a mistake. When money becomes the main object in life, then it takes away from the living of life."

LIFE'S MOST UNDERRATED: "Manners. I was brought up strictly, and it has stood me well. Manners are a matter of respect—one human being to another. It's a very under-taught part of life, one we should emphasize more."

GETTING WHAT YOU WANT: "You don't hear so much about people with dreams today. It's almost as if they're afraid to discover what they're individually capable of and would rather just follow the other fellow. But all of us have more inside us than we believe possible. Dream big and dare to fail."

Sanford Specht, 80

Somewhat sheepishly, Sanford Specht admits that he doesn't like to take off his shirt when he's on the beach in Florida. From hitting the heavy bag and lifting weights four days a week at a Manhattan gym, he's developed a physique that could make older women swoon.

A designer, inventor, and entrepreneur who has yet to retire, Specht has two daughters. But it was his 19-year-old grandson who inspired him to get back in shape at age 63. Today, they spot for each other in the gym, and Specht is writing a book called *Younger and Stronger*.

FRIENDSHIP: "If you have four or five real friends, you've

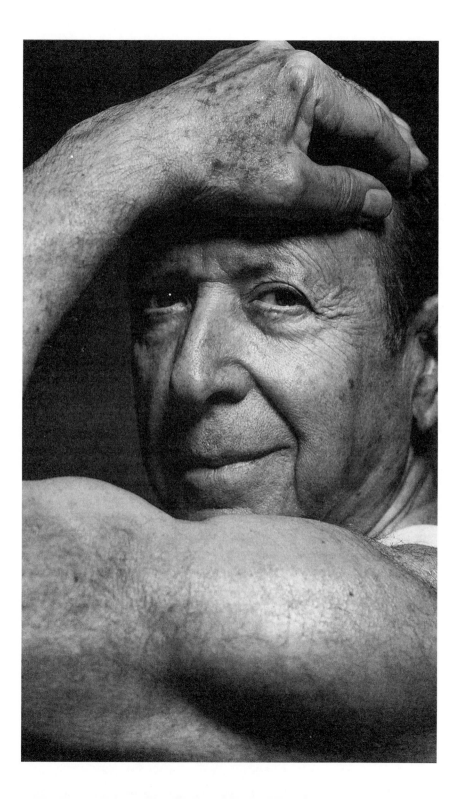

done a great job. Most 'friends' are just acquaintances. Life is like an octopus; you go in so many directions. You see some people every day for years, but your values change. Change is how you measure a friend—if he's still there through it all. I also try to have young friends. I'm selling my apartment in Florida because there's a lack of enthusiasm there. My wife and I go out with couples in their fifties, and their minds aren't young enough."

FAILURE: "It builds character. If you can step back, evaluate it, and determine what went wrong, you'll be a better person because of it."

LIFE'S MOST OVERRATED: "Wealth without health."

CAREER: "Be an explorer. Don't get into just one niche. I worked in California, Florida, Europe, and now Manhattan. Perhaps I could have made more money if I did just one thing, but that was never it. It's variety. It's the excitement of it all."

REMINISCING: "If you talk about the past too much, you won't have a future."

MOST PRECIOUS: "My health. When you have that, you can do everything. You can give people love. You can be interesting. My father died of a heart attack at 50. No man thinks he'll outlive his father. I thought I was going at 49. But here I am. No doubt about it, health is the most precious commodity."

SEX: "Sex is one of the most powerful things in the world. It's needed and wanted. But you need a relationship to go with it. Without that, it isn't meaningful."

THOUGHT IT MATTERED, BUT IT DOESN'T: "Fame. You reach a certain place with a certain degree of fame, but then it's always, 'Where do I go from here?' Family, friends—that's who you should work to be famous with."

Chapter 9

Everything Else

My father had two little black books, each a pocket-size binder into which he copied hundreds of favorite quotations, many of which you've already read in this book. They were written perfectly in his tiny script, almost as if for a period of his life he fancied himself a monk preserving the wisdom of the ages. They were never meant to be published, though. They were for his satisfaction and meditation alone. He never showed or explained them to me. For all the time I lived at home, they just sat on his bookshelf, an unexplored mystery.

"If you see someone without a smile, give them one of yours."

"The big shots are only the little shots who keep shooting."

"The only safe and sure way to destroy an enemy is to make him your friend."

The day he died, I finally opened them. Hoping to hear his voice one more time, desperate to gain insight into the man who had given me life yet never clearly explained it, I read. And in the next three hours, I'm embarrassed to admit, I learned more about my father than in the previous 32 years.

"The wise man thinks everything he says; the fool says everything he thinks."

"*To have what we want is riches, but to be able to do without is power.*"

"*The best thing to do behind a person's back is to pat it.*"

When you write something down to preserve it, you also absorb it. Each of the quotations in these journals, from sources as diverse as Socrates and the Pennsylvania Dutch, had given him pause—first when he came across it and then when he transcribed it. Each was meaningful to him. Each shaped him. Each, in some small way, was him.

"*The first step to greatness is to be honest.*"

"*It often shows a fine command of the language to say nothing.*"

"*The greatest truths are the simplest, and so are the greatest men.*"

These were the important things he must have wanted to tell me, only he couldn't put them in his own words, and he knew I wouldn't tolerate being lectured with someone else's. I can see that he tried to live out many of them, to personify what was being professed. And maybe that was the plan: to try showing me through example first, knowing that if he failed or if I never noticed, these books would one day make things clear.

"*A hero is one who knows how to hang on one minute longer.*"

"*It's not the years in your life that counts, but the life in those years.*"

"*This is the final test of a gentleman: his respect for those who can be of no possible service to him.*"

The unnerving thing is, the books still even smell like him—a musty mixture of Old Spice, garden dirt, and beer. Paging through one is like sitting next to him on the couch as a boy. And it's just as comforting. To hold one in my hand is to know that my dad is still there to guide me, to tell me what to do when I feel directionless.

"*No man is ever a failure until his wife thinks so.*"

"*No rule for success will ever work if you don't.*"

"*The grand essentials to happiness in this life are: something to do, something to love, and something to hope for.*"

Some days at work when my time seems wasted or stress has

almost paralyzed me, I pick up one of his books, close my eyes, and open to a random page. I imagine I've asked him a question and, from afar, he's sent a reply. Sometimes the advice is applicable. Most times it's not. But I feel better nonetheless.

"Studying all the angles keeps you from running around in circles."

"If you wish to succeed in managing and controlling others, learn to manage and control yourself."

"It is better to wear out than to rust out."

For a while, as a sort of prayer before my family's evening meal, I would have my children pick a quotation from his books and read it aloud. With hands joined, we'd ponder what was said and remind ourselves that it was only Pop Pop's body that was dead.

"Teach the young people how to think, not what to think."

"Next to excellence is the appreciation of it."

"To get nowhere, follow the crowd."

At his funeral, I carried these books with me on the long, lonely walk from pew to podium. I held them up, just like some preacher wielding the Bible, and I quoted my father's scripture to his congregation of friends. They, too, had never heard him utter these words but, now reminded, they all saw that he had lived them.

"You can preach a better sermon with your life than with your lips."

"Life is a mirror. If you frown at it, it frowns back. If you smile, it returns the greeting."

"To live a good saying is even better than merely writing it."

At the cemetery, as his casket was lowered and my mother's weeping rose, I touched one of his books in my breast pocket. It was proof that he was not gone, that he could not be buried entirely. I had, next to my heart, a piece of his soul.

"A good scare is worth more to a man than good advice."

"It is the man who does not want to express an opinion whose opinions I want."

"No matter what your lot in life may be, build something on it."

I don't intend to make my children read the book that I've created—the one you're holding in your hands now. If curiosity prompts them to try, then so be it. But at their young ages, I doubt if they'll be able to digest what's here or if it's even possible for them to care. It's sufficient for me to know that there will be a copy on my bookshelf so that the day I die, when they finally get the urge to know me better, they'll be able to sit down next to me on their couches, feel comforted, and listen.

"What a different world this would be if people would listen to those who know more and not merely try to get something from those who have more."

"You can't stop people from thinking, but you can start them."

HOW TO GET A BAT OUT OF YOUR HOUSE

"Just open the door and wait. Bats aren't as blind as you think, plus they sense temperature variations easily. Not only that, but they want out of the house as badly as you want them out. As with lingering relatives, sometimes you just have to show them the door."

—DENIS BOYLES, 52, PROFESSOR, WRITER, FARMER,
AND FATHER TO THREE

ACQUIRING PATIENCE

"Patience is being able to understand the other person's perspective. For instance, one day a nearby road was being paved, and my boys came home covered with oil and tar. They were about five at the time. They had on shorts and white T-shirts, and they were black. All I could see was their eyes. Well, I looked at them, and my first reaction was anger. But then I looked at them some more and realized how much fun they had been having. I think that's the essence of patience. You have to take a few seconds before you react and try to see where the other person is coming from."

—VINCE SPERRAZZA, 52, TECHNICIAN AND FATHER TO FOUR

DEALING WITH DISCRIMINATION

"I was an angry 18-year-old when I was put in a Japanese-American internment camp prior to World War II. I kept asking myself, 'What's happening?' But after awhile, I realized that whoever had made this decision didn't know me, and they didn't know the Japanese people. It was simple ignorance that made them do this. And that's what helped me handle it. I saw that it was stupidity, not hate."
—HENRY IKEMOTO, 74, RETIRED PROBATION OFFICER
AND FATHER TO FOUR

HOW TO GET NOTICED

"You can always get more accomplished by being humorous and a little eccentric because that's what gets people's attention. If you're too serious, people won't listen to you. Better to be different and interesting and get under their skin a bit."
—BOB MCCOY, 71, CURATOR OF THE MUSEUM
OF QUESTIONABLE MEDICAL DEVICES AND FATHER TO THREE

DISSATISFACTION

"I never want to be satisfied. I think being satisfied is pretty close to being dead. Everybody owes themselves a little dissatisfaction. Enjoy what you have, of course, but always be striving to make things a little better."
—FRANK EINTERZ, 70, RETIRED VICE-PRESIDENT
OF A FOOD-PROCESSING PLANT AND FATHER TO 13

ORGANIZING YOUR LIFE

"It's easy. First plan your work, then work your plan."
—RICHARD MOORE JR. (1923–1996), FINANCIAL MANAGER
AND FATHER TO FOUR

From My Father's Journal

"A friend is one who is as willing to help you when you need it as when you do not." —STUART W. KNIGHT

❧

"Everything is simpler than you think and more complex than you imagine." —GOETHE

❧

"Time is a friend—don't kill it."

❧

"The best thing about the future is that it only comes one day at a time."

❧

"Oddly enough, it's the person who knows everything who has the most to learn."

❧

"Monuments? What are they? The very pyramids have forgotten their builders. Deeds, not stones, are true monuments." —MOTLEY

❧

"Really important people seldom have time to act important."

❧

"You must write not so that you can be understood but so that you cannot possibly be misunderstood."

Fate

"If you watch the doors that have closed, you won't see the ones that are opening. Right after World War II, my boss called me in and said that the company was downsizing, so I was out of a job. But he told me that they were looking for engineers over at Lockheed. So I went there, and I'm sitting in this group, and I notice this girl walking down the aisle. I ask the fella next to me who she is, and he says her name is Margie. Turns out it's his girlfriend's girlfriend. Of course, the jungle drums start beating, and I mention I'd like to meet her. Well, we were married within the year, and it's been wonderful. The day I lost my job turned out to be the greatest day of my life."

—BILL BELL, 75, RETIRED MARKETING EXECUTIVE,
HUSBAND FOR 52 YEARS, AND FATHER TO THREE

Why Anger Is Good

"I have a terrible temper. I'm not violent, but I will speak my mind very quickly and loudly. I don't think anger is always a bad thing, though. Certainly, if it's going to cause you a heart attack or hurt somebody beyond repair, then it's not good. But if you don't feel anger, it probably means that you don't have any conviction, or at least not enough to let somebody know in no uncertain terms that you believe in this. So anger, to a certain extent, is good."

—RALPH HAAS, 63, RETIRED RADIO DISC JOCKEY, AUTHOR,
AND FATHER TO TWO

Smarts

"You don't have to be smart to be honest. But you have to be smart to be crooked."

—RUBEN DOMINGUEZ, 86, RETIRED MANUAL LABORER
AND FATHER TO FOUR

HOW TO CATCH MORE FISH THAN YOUR BUDDY

"Rub a little gasoline on your hands, then ask your buddy if you can check out his lures. 'Wow, these are beautiful,' you can say while you're fondling them. Most fish are smart when it comes to aromas. They hate the smell of gasoline. It's repulsive to them. Use a bit and it's guaranteed your friend won't catch a fish all day. Then wash your hands and rub them with a little peppermint oil to make your own lures more attractive."

—HOMER CIRCLE, 84, FISHERMAN, EDITOR, AND FATHER TO ONE

BEING A GOOD BOSS

"Some managers expect their employees to make them successful. I never approached it that way. In fact, I came at it from the opposite direction. I figured if I encouraged each of my employees to be successful, then I would just naturally be successful along with them. If you approach it this way, if you don't just think of yourself, then you'll be a successful manager."

—LOU PATTON, 70, RETIRED MANAGER FOR A COMPUTER FIRM AND FATHER TO THREE

COOL

"Cool guys never think 'cool.' But guys who aren't cool think about little else. The less cool they have, the harder they try. This gap between real coolness and wannabe coolness grows until the entire facade collapses, and you end up amidst the rubble of who you really are."

—DENIS BOYLES, 52, PROFESSOR, WRITER, FARMER, AND FATHER TO THREE

WAR

"At first, war was a big game to me. Until one day in Vietnam, I went ashore with some Marines, and they flushed out this girl and her baby. They yelled for her to stop running, but she didn't, and our point man shot her. The bullet just grazed her, but it cut off the baby's arm. It was hanging by the skin. It never registered in my mind until then that children are killed in wars. And to me, the war was over right there. War is useless. There are other ways to handle things."

—WESLEY PATTERSON, 66, CONSTRUCTION SUPERINTENDENT, VIETNAM VETERAN, AND FATHER TO FOUR

LIFE'S NEXT MOVE

"Anything I ever learned comes down to something pretty simple: Don't anticipate life; meet it. When you try to anticipate, you're being an idiot because nobody's got the brain to outwit nature. I'm talking here about patience, about believing in yourself. I'm talking here about having the courage to wait. You will get what you deserve."

—ROD STEIGER, 73, OSCAR-WINNING ACTOR AND FATHER TO ONE

BEING A SUCCESSFUL POLITICIAN

"Dreams are okay, but only to a certain point. Poetry is beautiful, but it cannot change people's lives. Unless we exchange political dreams and poetic speeches for practicality and fact, the world will continue to struggle. You should not promise in politics something that cannot be delivered by government."

—RICARDO SUAREZ, 56, ATTORNEY, EL SALVADOR PRESIDENTIAL CANDIDATE, AND FATHER TO THREE

Getting Out of Bed

"Waking up is a hallway that we typically rush through. But grogginess is actually an interesting type of consciousness. The time between sleep and wakefulness has great potential for creativity because you're so closely connected to the subconscious. Just return to the last position that you were sleeping in before you awoke, close your eyes, and hang there for 5 to 10 minutes. Notice the feelings and images that come."
—Rubin Naiman, Ph.D., 49, clinical health psychologist and father to three

Creating Art

"Don't be afraid to do something different. I have painted on everything you could imagine—canvas, wood, even slate that I've found in the mountains. Keep an open mind. Always be searching for a unique way to express what's inside you."
—Tom Haggard, 63, retired teacher and coach, artist, and father to two

How to Flirt

"The fleeting glance is the most effective way to flirt. The idea is to catch her eye, then look away, as if her beauty has nearly blinded you. Then glance back—*because you cannot help yourself.*"
—Robert Masello, from his book *The Things Your Father Never Taught You*

How to Change the World

"When you're in traffic, let the other guy in."
—John Heiser, M.D., 66, physician, clinical professor of anesthesia, and father to five

From My Father's Journal

"Everybody is ignorant, only on different subjects."
—WILL ROGERS

❧

"Life is too short to be little."

❧

"When you encounter a man of rare intellect, ask him what books he reads."

❧

"The great thing in the world is not so much where we stand, as in what direction we are moving."

❧

"He who overcomes by force has overcome but half his foe."

❧

"The real test in golf and in life is not in keeping out of the rough, but in getting out after we are in."

❧

"The selection of the right word calls for the exercise of man's greatest faculty—that of judgement."

❧

"Courage consists not in blindly overlooking danger, but in seeing it and conquering it."

Why Humble Men Are Great

"The world sees humility as a weakness, but it's really a strength. I mean, if you're not standing up for yourself, if you're not projecting yourself, if you're not being proactive, you're seen as a wimp. But really, it's an inner strength. You don't need to show others how powerful you are. And therein lies the greatness of humility."

—Vince Sperrazza, 52, technician and father to four

How to Control Your Temper

"Picture yourself standing opposite a guy who is six-foot-eight, weighs 300 pounds, and has fists the size of hams. You probably wouldn't lose your temper with him. Now if you can exercise that kind of control then, you can exercise that type of control anywhere."

—Frank Einterz, 70, retired vice-president
of a food-processing plant and father to 13

The Best Part of Being Sober

"I was an alcoholic for many years. I was like another person when I was drunk. My wife and kids never knew whether Godzilla was going to come flying through the window, or if I was going to come home in shackles with my nose broken, or if I was going to come home at all. I finally went to see an addictions therapist. I was 40, and I haven't had a drink since. You know the best part about being sober? The real reward is not seeing the fear in my children's eyes that I used to see whenever I walked into the room."

—Ozzy Osbourne, 50, rock star and father to four

HOW TO SPOT A LIAR

"Watch for two things: One, when he hesitates to answer a question he shouldn't have to think about, like, 'What did you do last night?' And two, any discrepancy between his face, voice, and body language. For instance, when his speech doesn't match his facial expression or when his body language doesn't fit his voice."

—PAUL EKMAN, PH.D., 63, PSYCHOLOGIST, FBI CONSULTANT, AUTHOR OF *TELLING LIES*, AND FATHER TO TWO

FINDING THE PLACE WHERE YOU BELONG

"My wife and I grew up in Ohio. We were both teachers, and we enjoyed the outdoors—hiking, camping, that sort of thing. So we took six weeks one summer, even though we couldn't afford it, and drove all around Montana, Wyoming, and Colorado. Basically, we were looking for a place to move—a small town near the mountains with a college where we could pursue our master's degrees. We found all that in Montrose, Colorado, and we've been here ever since. Finding the place where you belong is the same as finding who you are."

—FRED MATHENY, 53, WRITER, FORMER ENGLISH TEACHER, AND FATHER TO ONE

MASTERING FATIGUE

"Fatigue is much more mental than physical. If you believe that being up lots of hours will rob you of strength and energy, then it will. Try not to dwell on it. If you get only three hours of sleep, don't look back and say, 'Today is going to be tough because I didn't get enough rest.' Instead, think ahead and say, 'Okay, what is it I'm going to do today?'"

—JEFF LINDER, 52, COMMERCIAL AIRLINE PILOT AND FATHER TO ONE

Defending Your Country

"In order to live in a country where you have freedom and rights, you must be willing to fight for it. Because when you defend your country, you are, in fact, defending your home. A man who refuses to do that deserves no respect. Country is separate from government, though. Lots of people don't have much use for the federal government; they think it's a terrible bureaucracy. But country is different. It's the people, your neighbors, your common beliefs. That's what's worth fighting for."

—Jim Gordon, 61, Vietnam veteran, nurse, substance
abuse counselor, and father to three

Midlife Crisis: The Opportunity

"It feels kind of like when you were 16 or 17 years old, and you were in that awkward stage of life when you're no longer a boy but not yet a man. You're in between. It's very similar to that. You feel a sense of physical, mental, and spiritual change, but you're not quite sure where it's going. You feel like you're growing yet again."

—Vince Sperrazza, 52, technician and father to four

Midlife Crisis: The Threat

"A lot of men's midlife crisis stems from the fact that they're doing something they don't really like. They're looking ahead at the next 10 years and seeing a dead end. Either they're in a bad marriage or a bad job. If this describes you, don't wait for it to happen."

—Woodson Merrell, M.D., 50, integrative physician,
professor of medicine, and father to two

How to Be More Forgiving

"If you can forgive the first guy who messes with you each day, then the second guy is easier."
—HENRY IKEMOTO, 74, RETIRED PROBATION OFFICER
AND FATHER TO FOUR

The Scariest Thing about Growing Up

"Adulthood means never getting to say 'it's not my fault.'"
—FRANK PITTMAN III, M.D., 62, PSYCHIATRIST, AUTHOR
OF *GROW UP!*, AND FATHER TO THREE

Why You Should Always Risk It

"We were made to chase lions. But now we sit at computers and drive cars. When life gets boring, there's a natural need to take risks. I like to ski fast and drive even faster. If I had nine lives like a cat, I would have already used up five. But if you don't take risks, you don't get anywhere. Life is a risk."
—DON RANNEY, M.D., 67, PROFESSOR EMERITUS OF ANATOMY
AND KINESIOLOGY AND FATHER TO FOUR

Winning a Fistfight

"Feign insanity. Just go berserk. Many assaults are abandoned by the bad guy when he realizes that the price of victory is just too high. Or do the opposite: retreat, surrender, white-flag it. Start preaching the Bible's good news. He'll back off pronto."
—DENIS BOYLES, 52, PROFESSOR, WRITER, FARMER,
AND FATHER TO THREE

From My Father's Journal

"There are two kinds of people on Earth—the people who lift and the people who lean."

❦

"A wise man will make more opportunities than he finds." —FRANCIS BACON

❦

"Men are born with two eyes but with one tongue in order that they should see twice as much as they say."

❦

"The recollection of quality remains long after the price is forgotten."

❦

"There is so much good in the worst of us, and so much bad in the best of us, that it behooves all of us not to talk about the rest of us." —ROBERT LOUIS STEVENSON

❦

"When we say that a man has no sense of humor, what we really mean is that he hasn't the same sense of humor we have." —FRANK CASE

❦

"Trying to keep a good man down is about as hard as trying to keep a good-for-nothing one up."

The Best Defense? A Good Attack

"The best way to win a fight is to try to avoid it. But if that doesn't work, then you better make sure you deliver the first punch."

—Ruben Dominguez, 86, retired manual laborer
and father to four

How to Get Rid of Guilt

"If you're feeling guilty about something, the best thing you can do is go explain it to somebody. Find a confidante, someone you respect and say, 'Hey, I did something that wasn't right. What do you think I should do?' Some people keep it to themselves, and it just burns within them."

—Paul Woehlke, 56, hospital administrator
and father to two

Temptation

"It's important that you give in to some temptations so that you can see what temptation is, what it does, and how there's usually a real sense of emptiness afterward. We really have no right to say to anyone that he shouldn't be checking these things out. If you want to try something, go ahead. That's your choice. That's your freedom. Just be wise enough to realize that there are some temptations you may never come back from."

—Jeff Linder, 52, commercial airline pilot
and father to one

Keeping a Clean Nose

"To stay out of trouble, stay sober. You have no judgment when you're not. Listen to your instincts, too. If you know it's not quite right to cheat on your taxes or fudge on a loan application, then don't do it. That's the start of trouble."

—Aaron Binder, 70, entrepreneur, ex-con,
and father to two

R-E-S-P-E-C-T

"Staying out of trouble is simple. It's a matter of having respect—for yourself, for other people, and for other people's property."

—ALFRED WILLIAMS, 64, FORMER PRESIDENT COUNTY JUDGE
AND FATHER TO THREE

HOW TO GET INTO A FANCY NIGHTCLUB

"Skip the line. Instead, walk a few blocks until you find an expensive hotel. Hang out until a limousine pulls up. (If your wait is more than a half-hour, then you didn't pick the right hotel.) After the driver lets the passengers out, offer him $20 to give you a ride around the corner to the nightclub. Hesitate for a few minutes before you make your exit. Then just walk toward the door as if there's no question that you'll be let in. If there is a question, answer in French."

—DENIS BOYLES, 52, PROFESSOR, WRITER, FARMER,
AND FATHER TO THREE

WORRY

"My grandmother always used to say, 'Worry is like a rocking chair. It keeps you busy, but it don't get you nowhere.'"

—WILL HESS, 70, RETIRED RAILROAD WORKER
AND FATHER TO FOUR

HOW TO APOLOGIZE

"If finding the appropriate words is always hard for you, just keep it simple. Try something like this: 'I'm so sorry for what happened on Saturday. I hope you'll accept my apology.'"

—ROBERT MASELLO, FROM HIS BOOK *THE THINGS YOUR
FATHER NEVER TAUGHT YOU*

WHAT CAUSES LONELINESS

"Some people complain, 'Oh, I'm so lonely.' Well, hey, that's your own doing. Don't blame it on anybody else. I live by myself, but I'm not lonely. I have books and music galore. I'm handy, so I create things. I have dreams. I have ideas."
—H. T. BREMER, 64, CONSTRUCTION ENGINEER AND FATHER TO FOUR

WHY BEING RIGHT IS WRONG

"It is wrong to be right; it puts other people down and keeps you from learning anything new. Practice telling people that you may be wrong about the subject under discussion. Practice saying, 'I don't know. What do you think?' to your loved ones and those you care about. The rewards will amaze you."
—FRANK PITTMAN III, M.D., 62, PSYCHIATRIST, AUTHOR OF GROW UP!, AND FATHER TO THREE

HOW TO NEVER MAKE ANOTHER MISTAKE

"Don't use the word *mistake* anymore. Instead, call it a life experience. If you go at life for the right reasons and things don't go as planned, that's not a mistake. That's a life experience. You wouldn't be where you are today if you didn't go through that learning process—good or bad."
—VINCE SPERRAZZA, 52, TECHNICIAN AND FATHER TO FOUR

LOSING YOUR HAIR

"The first time I felt the urge to hide my growing bald spot, I bought a shaver and gave myself a military haircut. No hair to worry about: what a feeling of freedom. I've been bald for many years now. Do you think being hairless bothers me a little bit? Damn right it does. I hate being bald. But I hate it proudly."
—RANDY WAYNE WHITE, 48, FISHING GUIDE, WRITER, AND FATHER TO TWO

From My Father's Journal

"No one is exempt from talking nonsense; the misfortune is to do it solemnly." —MONTAIGNE

※

"The best time to make friends is before you need 'em."

※

"Each year, one bad habit rooted out, in time ought make the worst man good."

※

"Superior people talk about ideas, average people talk about things, and little people talk about other people."

※

"The magic formula in human relations is simple—when you begin to dislike someone, do something nice for him." —JOHN K. SHERMAN

※

"The nature of men is always the same; it's their habits that separate them." —CONFUCIUS

※

"The secret to success in conversation is to be able to disagree without being disagreeable."

※

"Common sense is not so common."

BEING REMEMBERED WELL

"The key is to help others in some way. I know that sounds like a cliché, but if you want to be remembered well by your friends and family, then you have to remember them well."
—FRED MATHENY, 53, WRITER, FORMER ENGLISH TEACHER, AND FATHER TO ONE

THE BEST KIND OF CHARITY

"Whenever you become really good at something, find a way to share it with other people."
—WESLEY PATTERSON, 66, CONSTRUCTION SUPERINTENDENT, VIETNAM VETERAN, AND FATHER TO FOUR

Epilogue

What I Know

My son, angered by one of my edicts, yelled in sarcastic defiance, "What do *you* know?" It felt like I had taken a right to the chin. I was momentarily staggered. If he had simply refused to listen, insisted that he was going to do what *he* wanted to do, I could have gotten angry and punished him. Even if his reply had been a tearful, "I hate you," I would have recognized it as adolescent emotion and been able to forgive. But this? To question my wisdom, my intelligence, struck at the very core of what I had always believed to be my chief duty as a dad. He had found and used four of the most hurtful words a father can hear. If a son has no respect for your knowledge, then what is left to be proud of? What can you give him that's of value, of substance, other than just your love?

What *do* I really know—without a doubt, for sure?

That's a difficult question that talking to the fathers in this book helped crystallize for me. As I mentioned at the outset, the majority of the dads I interviewed had never been asked these big questions of life, nor had they given much thought to the answers. While that's an embarrassment for us as children, it's also a reason to hang our heads as adults and parents. If we want to be bigger than life in the eyes of our offspring, then we have to ponder the big things in life. Success, God, sex, death—

all the chapter headings in this book and more. Just as we shouldn't hesitate to ask our fathers about them, we also shouldn't wait to form opinions and speak our minds when it comes to them.

I once worked for a man named Bob Rodale, who was as quiet, fragile, and unassuming as a detail is small. Yet he lived in the big picture, forever pondering issues such as health, environment, and regeneration. He was a local farmer and a global publisher, which speaks to the dichotomy within him. His feet were in the soil, but his head was in the heavens. He was an ordinary man with extraordinary thoughts. He was proof that the two can coexist.

Nevertheless, he was sometimes snickered at behind his back by the bean counters in his company, who found his projects too unprofitably grandiose. A velodrome in Pennsylvania. A farming magazine in Russia. A pedal-powered lawn mower. Some of the conventional thinkers who worked for Rodale just didn't understand his foresight. On more than one occasion, I heard them say, "What does *he* know?"

Ideas and opinions are like grass seed. You reach into your sack and throw out a handful to cover a bare spot. Whether any take hold depends on which way the wind is swirling, how rich the soil is, and if you're diligent enough to look after them. The spirit with which they're cast, however, always takes root and endures. That hope for change, that vision of vibrancy, is like a weed. Before long, it takes over. While many of Bob Rodale's individual ideas died with him in 1990, the hope, vision, and even eccentricity that birthed them continues to underlie and drive his company today.

Do you remember what it feels like to have a fresh idea? Can you recall the electricity that lightbulb generated in you, how time suddenly stood still, and how you suddenly couldn't?

That is the spirit of big thought. That is the excitement of enlightenment. What's remarkable is that this feeling isn't dependent on the uniqueness, validity, or even worth of your idea.

The reward arrives with the insight. And it is as addictive as it is life-altering. Once tasted, the brain craves and eventually obtains more.

A few years ago, I started keeping a "wisdom journal." Diaries had always stymied me (no secrets to confess, I guess), and exercise logs seemed pointless (why ledger what's meant to be fun?). But this was different. This was exciting. To write down, at the end of each day, something new I had learned or a fresh idea I'd had, made me feel like I was growing, or at least moving somewhere.

Indeed, I'm continually amazed at how many thoughts I have—ideas and musings that would have washed right past me if I weren't writing them down. It has convinced me that no man is a dullard, that every man is a philosopher. The difference is simply that wise men lecture or write, while dullards keep things to themselves. I think everyone should keep a journal like this— if not to know yourself, then so your children may one day know you better.

Harry Truman, president and father, once said, "It's what you learn after you know it all that counts."

For what it's worth, here are a few things I've learned, a few excerpts from my wisdom journal, a few truths I really do know. May they inspire a few of your own. I've even left you some space at the end.

How to Grow a Brain

Ask your kids big questions. Is there a God? Where do birds go to die? What makes you *you*? Even if they can't supply any answers, at least you'll have started them thinking.

The Secret to Everything

The key to success, happiness, and health is to do one thing, and only one thing, at a time.

HOW TO BE FOREVER YOUNG

To never age, always dream. Imagine places you want to go, second careers you'd like to start, things you want to buy. Dreaming keeps you moving forward, and even more important, it's the spark plug for learning. Before you take that trip to Australia, you'll read about it. Before you open that business, you'll study the market. And before you buy that computer, you'll try to understand how it works.

Let new dreams simmer like a good stew, but don't let them cook away to nothing. All dreams, no matter how outrageous, are actionable. Take small steps toward them, and you'll feel your life become more exciting and more purposeful.

THE BEST KIND OF DOCTOR

Pick a doctor who smiles a lot and has an optimistic disposition. Studies suggest that when people become seriously ill, a positive attitude on the part of their physicians often makes the difference.

TRUE GENIUS

Genius is another name for victory in the fight to be yourself. I write a story, and a dozen hands are at it, editing, shaping, and changing. The result is uniformity, an article that fits the voice and style of the publication in which it will appear. It becomes just another uniformed child in a prep school. To succeed, you must not only have ability but also the tenaciousness to not let your work be fit into some plan. Genius is creating something that doesn't fit, something totally unique.

WHEN YOUR SON WANTS TO STUDY ANTHROPOLOGY

Ever since I can remember, I wanted to be a writer. There must be thousands of careers that are more profitable, but my father never tried to steer me toward any of them. If it's in a child's heart to pursue something, then let him do it. Parenting isn't about interfering, it's about enabling.

HOW TO PICK A WINNER AT THE TRACK

A pile of horse manure weighs as much as 10 pounds. Consider a post-weigh-in dump the equivalent of a bonus handicap.

THE MOST DANGEROUS KIND OF WOMAN

Love is not a business plan. It can't be approached as a goal or a bottom line, where engagement is slated for the first quarter, marriage for the second, a home for the third, and kids for the close of the fiscal. Many never-married thirty-something women with ticking biological clocks approach it this way, though. Beware of them. For love to be true, it has to be largely unplanned. Scientists will never precipitate it in a test tube, and you'll never create it out of some pressing need. Love happens on its own and pays its own dividends. It is strongest and most enduring when it is magic.

HOW TO GET WHAT YOU WANT

When you want to get your way, simply try being mannerly. It's become so rare nowadays that it disarms people. It throws them off balance. Don't think of it as merely being nice; rather, consider it "civil" war.

THE FIRST RULE OF BEING A BOSS

To be an effective manager, don't get too close to those you supervise. You can be friendly, but you can't be friends. Otherwise, they won't respect you, and you won't be able to tell them the truth.

HEAVEN ON EARTH

There is a zone to writing. It takes some effort, some hours of struggle to reach, but once you're there, the words flow as if from a spigot. Thoughts fill up the page. Your fingers function independently of your body and brain as you tap out the poetry. It's the groove that baseball hitters speak of. The hot hand that basketball players relish. It is that sweet moment in a race car when everything slows down despite the speedometer reading 175 miles per hour. Everything doable in life has a zone like this. Find it and get into it.

LAST WORDS YOU SHOULDN'T UTTER

Men who proudly say that they have no regrets in life should be pitied, not praised. That means they were too careful; they didn't take enough chances.

PRUNING OLD BUDS

Old friends are precious, but if you're not careful, they will tether you to the past. New friends pull you away from what you were, force you to interact in fresh ways and, ultimately, teach you new things. Make sure your life is filled with both.

HOW TO AVOID AN ACCIDENT

No matter how clearly you think you see or how thorough you believe you've been, there's usually some part of the whole that you've missed. It's like the blind spot just over your left shoulder when you're driving a car. There is something unseen. With a parent, it might be his love. With a spouse, her boredom. With a child, his fear. Train yourself to take an extra second to look over your shoulder when you're merging into the world. It's so simple to do, but we're always in such a hurry, accelerating away. No wonder so many accidents happen.

THE BEST HALLOWEEN COSTUME

Never let your kids buy an off-the-shelf Halloween costume. Forbid it, no matter how close you may be to the witching hour. Instead, help them make their own. Encourage them to use their imaginations and their ingenuity. Show them that what can be created is often better than what can be bought. And besides, don't the darkest, most frightening things live inside us anyway?

TWO-MINUTE MARRIAGE COUNSELING

For the next two minutes, look at your partner. Don't speak, don't let anything distract you. Just study. For those who have been together for a long time, it's surprisingly tough to do—and remarkably stirring. This little exercise, when practiced periodically, will cure all your minor relationship woes. For more difficult problems, do this while making love.

BUILDING CONFIDENCE

Few of us can be perfect in the grand scheme, but everyone can be peerless when it comes to the particulars. Whether it's cutting the lawn, pressing a shirt, or even washing dishes, there's a satisfaction that springs from attending to little things and controlling what you can. It's not just relaxing, it builds pride. Confidence grows from a mastery of the mundane into a conviction that you can handle anything.

WHEN TO TAKE A PAY CUT

Even if you have to take a step down to get where the action is, do it. It's better to be the vice-president of an up-and-coming company than the president of a dying one.

HOW TO LOSE WEIGHT

The simplest, most effective way to lose weight is to eat with your opposite hand. It slows you down, encourages you to chew your food better, and makes you feel full sooner. This last effect stems from the fact that in recognizing fullness, our brains lag behind our stomachs by about 20 minutes. If you slow everything down, you'll eat less.

TAG-TEAM CHILD RAISING

If you want to be a good father, make sure your wife has a job—even if it's just part-time. Otherwise, being the lazy bum that you are, you'll probably let her feed the kids, play with them, tuck them into bed, and generally raise them. But if she's not around (an evening job is best), then you're the one who'll have to warm up their Spaghettios, set up Chutes and Ladders, and read them Dr. Seuss. It'll force you to be a dad.

A working wife also holds advantages for a marriage beyond just the extra cash. The less you see of someone, the more you appreciate them. It prevents "being together" from becoming a habit.

HOW TO TAKE YOUR VACATION

Don't take a solid week off from work. The days will rush together, and before you know it, it'll be gone. Instead, take half-days. When the temperature tops 60 for the first time in April, cut out at noon. When a late-September front sweeps through, leaving the air crisp and the sky sapphire blue, tell your boss that there's a pressing matter you must attend to. Taking half-days will help you be spontaneous, watchful of opportunities, and a treasurer of nature. That one balmy afternoon, that one fresh morning, those four glorious hours, will seem longer than any week. You'll do more, smile more, and refresh yourself more. It'll be like you cheated and didn't get caught—a quickie in the closet. Take all your vacation as half-days, and you'll lead a fuller life.

THE ULTIMATE EXERCISE

Although it doesn't involve moving one muscle, I've found this exercise harder (and ultimately, more beneficial) than lifting a stack of weights: Sit quietly for five minutes and think of nothing. Stop your conscious mind and just be. It's difficult to do at first, but with training, the power will come. What it does is rest your intellect, which rarely gets a break these days. You can exist without it. Try.

THE BEST QUALITY IN A MAN

There is no greater quality in a man than generosity. When you share something with another, you're putting that person and your friendship above any material good. That's the proper order of life.

WHEN FATHERHOOD HURTS MOST

The most difficult part of being a parent is waiting for your children to come home late at night. That's because they're out of your control. They are free. They are without you in their lives. And all you've taught them is being tested.

HOW TO BECOME A RICH MAN

It's the details of life that have the power to make a saw-buck like yourself feel like a million. A crisp, line-dried cotton bedsheet at the end of a hard day. Beer chilled to 38°F and served in a Pilsner glass. The diamond ankle bracelet you gave her sparkling above a stiletto heel. Most men are too busy to bother. Most men don't have the time to linger. But that is precisely the point. For those who do, that instant of satisfaction, that second of pleasure, is the moment of wealth.

THE THING TO FEAR MOST

I am afraid of lightning. I hide in a thunderstorm. But as much as I dread a blackening sky and a distant rumbling, I welcome the humbling. It is good for a man to be reminded that he can be struck down at any time, and that the taller and higher up he is, the more likely it is to happen. The moment you outgrow fear is the time to really be scared.

HOW TO SLOW DOWN TIME

Routines make people old and dull. Avoid them. This isn't to say that you should never marry or take a job. But rather, vary the routines within these bigger routines. If your work schedule is flexible, then go in at different times. Drive different routes. Eat lunch at two. Go to bed at nine. Do something spontaneous each day. Respond to an urge.

Routines are easy to follow. They demand no energy and little thought. They make time fly. To really live is to live unexpectedly.

WHY VIOLENCE IS AN OPPORTUNITY

Instead of shielding your children from the violence in movies and on television, watch it with them and explain the difference between fact and fiction, good and evil. I watch R-rated movies with my kids. I wince at the gunshots and gore, but before I tuck them into bed at night, I make sure that they understand the reality of what they just saw. There are lessons to be learned: that death is rarely dramatic, that guns are for the spineless, that blood is followed by tears. Your kids will eventually be exposed to this Hollywood nonsense on their own. Better to be with them the first few times it happens.

THE BEST WORKOUT

Working out is not the same as working. No matter how hard you ride that bike or lift those weights, it is something once removed from physical labor. And that's because working out doesn't accomplish anything tangible in a short amount of time. Even after a couple of hours, you're left with nothing you can see other than sweat. With physical labor, though, there is a reward, an immediate accomplishment. Toss 10 yards of mulch for eight hours and the body has a pleasant all-over ache, plus you're left with the satisfaction of looking at the black glow of your backyard. Labor is good for the soul. Fitness is just good for the muscles. The best way to work out is still to simply work.

HOW TO MAKE A DECISION

Learn to trust your instincts. After all, that's why they're called instincts—they're designed to help you flourish. Before you make a decision, stop your mind from meddling and check your gut feeling. All logic aside, when you first learned of the situation, what was your initial inclination?

That's what you should do.

WHY MEN LOOK AT OTHER WOMEN

Whenever I'm attracted to another woman, I pause for a moment and ask myself what it is about her that excites me. Usually, I find that she is tall, athletic, and leggy, with medium-length brown hair, dark eyes, and a generous smile. She is classy without being aloof, sweet without being a pushover. At some point during this inventory, it usually dawns on me that the reason I'm drawn to this woman is that she's very similar to my wife. She, in some small way, is just like her. So what's the point of chasing another when I've already found her?

HOW TO SAY GOOD NIGHT

The best thing you can do for your children is convince them that they can grow up to be anything they want. Sounds simple, but think about it. *Anything!* That's tremendously exciting, and it imparts a certain confidence. It's better than a bedtime story. Put them to sleep with the possibilities.

Some Space for Wisdom

228

Some Space for Wisdom

Some Space for Wisdom

230

Some Space for Wisdom

Some Space for Wisdom

232

Some Space for Wisdom